"If Christ is not raised from the dead, then our faith is worthless (1 Cor. 15:14). However, Christ is risen and lives today! Surprisingly, few good books have been written on the vital subject of Christ's resurrection, so Dr. Gabe Fluhrer's work is all the more welcome. This gripping, well-written book argues from the Holy Scriptures and from careful reasoning that Christ's resurrection is both true history and the ground of our hope both objectively and subjectively."

—Dr. Joel R. Beeke
President, Puritan Reformed Theological Seminary
Pastor, Heritage Reformed Congregation
of Grand Rapids, Mich.

"Dr. Gabe Fluhrer upholds the historical faith of Christianity in the physical resurrection of Jesus Christ from the dead. Its historical reality, for him, is the culmination of a much larger narrative, and its theological significance is inseparable from God's redemptive plan since the resurrection of Christ and the final resurrection of the dead are distinct episodes of the same event. From this perspective, Dr. Fluhrer examines and rejects the arguments raised by scholars against the physical resurrection of Jesus, explains the Old Testament promises that point to the resurrection, and shows how the resurrection was understood and applied by the New Testament authors. In addition to its apologetic character, this book has a pastoral and practical dimension, where it explores the implications of Christ's resurrection for the lives of believers. In a time of skepticism like ours, this book comes as a ray of faith and hope in the central event of Christianity."

—Dr. Augustus Nicodemus Lopes
Vice president of the Presbyterian Church of Brazil
Assistant pastor of First Presbyterian Church of Recife, Brazil

"The resurrection of Jesus Christ sits at the very heart of the gospel. What does it mean that Jesus was raised from the dead? How do we know that the resurrection is true? How does the resurrection help me face death? How does the resurrection help me to live my life today? With the mind and heart of a pastor and theologian, Dr. Gabe Fluhrer deftly walks us through the Bible to see the centrality, beauty, and glory of the resurrection. Indeed, he rightly says, 'For believers, the reality of Jesus' resurrection means that everything has changed.' Take up *Alive* and begin to see with fresh eyes what a difference the resurrection makes."

—Dr. Guy Prentiss Waters
James M. Baird Jr. Professor of New Testament
Reformed Theological Seminary, Jackson, Miss.

ALIVE

ALIVE

HOW *the* RESURRECTION *of* CHRIST

CHANGES EVERYTHING

GABRIEL N.E. FLUHRER

IR *Reformation Trust*   A DIVISION OF LIGONIER MINISTRIES, ORLANDO, FL

Alive: How the Resurrection of Christ Changes Everything
© 2020 by Gabriel N.E. Fluhrer

Published by Reformation Trust Publishing
a division of Ligonier Ministries
421 Ligonier Court, Sanford, FL 32771
Ligonier.org   ReformationTrust.com

Printed in Ann Arbor, Michigan
Cushing-Malloy, Inc.
0000221

ISBN 978-1-64289-240-6 (Paperback)
ISBN 978-1-64289-241-3 (ePub)
ISBN 978-1-64289-242-0 (Kindle)

Cover design: Ligonier Creative
Interior design and typeset: Katherine Lloyd, The DESK

Unless otherwise noted, Scripture quotations are from the ESV® Bible (The Holy Bible, English Standard Version®), copyright © 2001 by Crossway, a publishing ministry of Good News Publishers. Used by permission. All rights reserved.

Library of Congress Cataloging-in-Publication Data
Names: Fluhrer, Gabriel N. E., 1978- author.
Title: Alive : how the Resurrection of Christ changes everything /
    Gabriel N.E. Fluhrer.
Description: Orlando, FL : Reformation Trust Publishing, a division
    of Ligonier Ministries, [2020] | Includes bibliographical references. |
Identifiers: LCCN 2019033632 (print) | LCCN 2019033633 (ebook) |
    ISBN 9781642892406 (paperback) | ISBN 9781642892413 (epub) |
    ISBN 9781642892420 (kindle edition)
Subjects: LCSH: Jesus Christ--Resurrection--Biblical teaching. |
    Jesus Christ--Historicity. | Bible--Evidences, authority, etc.
Classification: LCC BT482 .F58 2020 (print) | LCC BT482 (ebook) |
    DDC 232/.5--dc23
LC record available at https://lccn.loc.gov/2019033632
LC ebook record available at https://lccn.loc.gov/2019033633

CONTENTS

INTRODUCTION

We have been told, over and over again, that life in the West has never been more secular. Pundits insist that what remains of our Christian heritage resembles the now-vacant cathedrals that haunt our urban centers or the fast-emptying rural churches sprinkled throughout the so-called flyover states: irrelevant, crumbling, and abandoned.

Despite this well-worn narrative, a closer look reveals that secularism's victory dance is premature. A strong argument could be (and has been) made that never before have we lived in a more spiritual age.[1] Modern man tolerates and even embraces the supernatural. From horoscopes to omens to fate to fascination with ghost stories to a vague deistic hope that the "big man upstairs" is looking out for us, the atheistic dream of a world shorn of belief in the sacred is dying more rapidly than the Christian worldview it sought to replace.

On a popular level, people remain stubbornly committed to the reality of a world beyond nature. Even the best efforts of a bloated and biased scientific establishment to disabuse them of such antiquated fantasies have not changed their minds.

But this entrenched commitment to the reality of the beyond

should not cause the Christian to rejoice. Rather, it should be a source of great sadness. Although Christians can celebrate the long-overdue rejection of the cold, hopeless, antisupernatural worldview of the atheistic establishment, they must simultaneously mourn the corresponding rise of the nebulous spiritualism of the present.

We must mourn this "spiritualism" because not all spiritualism is created equal. In other words, the supernatural world described by the Bible—in which God is sovereign—is not the same as horoscopes, fate, or deism.

The modern secularist may tolerate some form of spiritualism, at least in a general sense, but he will presumably never accept a supernaturalism that claims absolute authority over his life. In fact, as has been the case throughout the woeful history of our fallen race, the worldly mind will consistently take up arms against this kind of claim. It will march proudly into an ideological battle against any demand for its unqualified allegiance.

The resurrection of Christ represents just such a claim of absolute authority. As luminous as the first beams of sunshine that brightened Jerusalem the first Easter morning two thousand years ago, the light of Christ's victory over the grave scatters the drowsy pagan gloom of the present. Jesus' resurrection represents the highest sort of supernaturalism, but in a *supportive* fashion (more on this below).

By stating the matter this way, I am not at all claiming that the historical reality of the resurrection of Jesus is thereby unimportant—far from it, as I will argue at length in what follows. It is of supreme importance. But the biblical writers did not share the skepticism of miracles that has anesthetized the West since the Enlightenment. Therefore, they did not encounter the same hurdles to belief in the resurrection that might cause someone today to stumble.

For the writers of the New Testament, at least two astonishing, revolutionary, world-changing facts emerged from the empty tomb of Christ. First, according to the Apostles, the resurrection of Christ as a physical miracle in the space-time continuum was simply the culmination of a series of miraculous interventions by the Creator of the universe, going all the way back to the dawn of history. We will discuss this statement in more detail in chapter 2. For the moment, we only wish to point out that the *physical fact* of the resurrection was *supportive* of a far greater narrative. Therefore, in the second place, the God-intended *meaning* of the resurrection of Christ was paramount for the Apostles. The *historical reality* thus plays a supporting role to the *theological meaning* of that first Easter morning. Both, however, are indispensable: the historical reality of Jesus' resurrection and its theological meaning are inseparable and essential parts of God's redemptive plan.

Before proceeding, let me briefly discuss our terms. The resurrection refers, first and foremost, to the resurrection of Christ from the dead (see Matt. 28:1ff; Mark 16:1ff; Luke 24:1ff; John 20:1–10). The word can also refer to a more general event that will take place at the end of time, namely, the reunion of body and soul for all who have ever lived, for good or for ill (see Dan. 12:2; Matt. 25:31–46; John 5:25–29). As Paul explains in 1 Corinthians 15:20, our Lord's victory over the grave was the "firstfruits" of a general resurrection harvest. His resurrection is thus the precursor to a more general, future occurrence.

In thinking about *resurrection*, the term *event* may be too generic, resulting in an unhelpful ambiguity. As one scholar explains, Christ's resurrection and the resurrection of all people at the end of time should not be construed as two separate *events*. Rather, they are two *episodes* of the same event, even if they are separated by thousands of years.[2] Stated more simply, Christ's resurrection, as *the* resurrection, is the guarantor and beginning of *our* resurrection, to our everlasting delight or terror. Because these are distinct yet inseparable episodes,[3] the firstfruits implies and guarantees the harvest. More on this in chapter 6.

With this in mind, we cannot think about the resurrection of Christ without also seeing the more general resurrection on the horizon. To deny one is to deny the other. To affirm one is to affirm the other. This book will focus primarily on Christ's resurrection.

In addition, the argument here is not that other religions or worldviews do not affirm a resurrection of some variety. There are a handful that do. But they are nothing like the biblical view. This is because, again, the resurrection of Christ as a *historical* reality has a deeply *theological* meaning, one that is incomprehensible apart from the worldview to which it is connected.

In what follows, I will begin by demonstrating the historical fact of Christ's bodily resurrection. This will occupy our attention in the first and second chapters. We will examine some objections raised by scholars who deny that Jesus rose from the grave. I think the resurrection of Christ is so well attested historically that the objections raised against it are persuasive only to those who have already made up their minds. In other words, the faith of those who reject the resurrection, while mistaken and misplaced, is every bit as firm as that of those who embrace the resurrection.

The bulk of our study will concentrate on the biblical materials themselves. We will explore the promises and foreshadowings of Christ's resurrection in the Old Testament. Admittedly, the resurrection was only whispered to the saints who lived before Jesus' first coming. What was a whisper to those living under the old covenant becomes a deafening roar for the New Testament authors.

Accordingly, we will spend a few chapters exploring what the Gospels, the book of Acts, and the rest of the New Testament teach concerning Jesus' resurrection and therefore our resurrection. Finally, we will conclude by drawing some (I hope, practical and pastoral) conclusions regarding what the reality of resurrection means for our day-to-day lives.

My goal is for the reader to gain an appreciation for, a wonder at, and an enjoyment of the stupendous truth that sets Christianity apart from other world religions, namely, the reality that Jesus Christ is alive. Yes, as the Apostles' Creed confesses, He was buried. So were Muhammad, Buddha, and countless other religious leaders. But the next line of the ancient creed, simple in expression yet enormous in implication, is what I hope to expound, examine, and, most importantly, adore along with you in the pages that follow: "The third day he rose again from the dead."

One of the scholars whose arguments we will scrutinize in chapter 1 is Bart Ehrman, best-selling author and professor at the University of North Carolina at Chapel Hill. He fancies himself unshackled from the restrictive fundamentalism of his naive youth, and he wants the reader to join the agnostic exodus with him. Hence, he begins his popular-level books with his *de*conversion testimony. If he, as a secular intellectual, is permitted to do that, then I will offer my conversion testimony without apology.

During my senior year at the University of South Carolina, I found myself in a familiar place for a soon-to-be college grad. As my undergraduate days drew to a close, I was unsure of what I believed, but I was certain that what I had labeled "fundamentalist Christianity" (which I have since come to understand was simply the historic Christian faith) was unworthy of being taken seriously by thinking people. Sure, we went to a mainline church growing up (who didn't go to some kind of church in South Carolina?), but I had given myself to the study of philosophy. I read the great texts, tried to think critically, and shut myself up to the fact that I was on my own in the quest for truth.

Indeed, the very quest for *truth* with a definite article was something I needed to abandon as a mark of intellectual maturity. An inerrant book? The leftovers of a modernist, quasi-adolescent yearning for certitude. Better to live with ambiguity than sacrifice the intellect on the altar of a naive certainty. Only one way to heaven, through the blood sacrifice of Jesus? An arrogant, bigoted claim that is not only repulsive in its exclusivity but laughable to anyone who has lived outside the confines of a comfortable, Christian-influenced culture.

Rather, I had concluded that the world was a complicated, big place. I still believe this, perhaps more so since I became a Christian. However, I thought, exclusive claims like those I had heard from "fundamentalist" Christians could be dismissed safely.

Then, after I graduated, I began to examine some of the evidence for the resurrection because of a book I came across called *The Case for Christ.* In my arrogance, I argued that this was a book for a popular audience, not a scholarly work, so I could still keep it at arm's length. But the thinkers to whom Lee Strobel introduced me revealed a side of Christianity I had never encountered, both because of my ignorance and because of my own love of sin.

Strobel's book featured serious Christian scholarship presented at a popular level. So I read rebuttals to Strobel's work. And I continued reading Christian scholars who defended one doctrine on which I knew the whole system turned: the resurrection of Christ.

Like most students and graduates, I was agnostic about the miraculous. But the more I studied, the more I realized that if Jesus is alive (that is, if His resurrection is a historical fact), then I could no longer ignore Him. Therefore, I examined the evidence for the resurrection and Christianity with something of a single-minded devotion. I looked at different denominations. I spoke with whomever I could about my questions. I read and reread, all the while making notes in the margins.

Two things happened during this time, both unforgettable to me. First, I was overwhelmed by the evidence for Christ's resurrection. I realized that my bias toward the miraculous was just that: a bias, not a solid argument. As we will see in chapter 1, I have since come to realize that, despite the hand waving and posturing of the scholarly establishment, an unwarranted antisupernatural bias infects academia.

But once that bias was overcome, one fact became as plain as the fall sunlight that warmed my neck as I studied: the resurrection of Christ happened. It wasn't a hallucination. It wasn't the deepest spiritual longings of man realized in some sort of "Easter event," as some biblical scholars in the twentieth century argued. It was real.

I was ruined. If the resurrection was true, and I had come to see that it was, then the skepticism of my college years was unfounded. But I wasn't ready to commit myself wholeheartedly to Christ yet.

So, in the second place, I began to listen to Dr. R.C. Sproul's radio program *Renewing Your Mind*. I had no idea what the Reformed faith was; I had just started to believe that miracles like the resurrection could happen. But I listened to Dr. Sproul every morning in my old truck tooling around the Upcountry of South Carolina.

He explained the gospel to me, not in broad strokes but in specifics that at once both wounded and cured my soul. What was a vague ache of conscience crystallized into radical depravity. I knew that I was enslaved to desires and habits and that I was, in sum, in rebellion against the living and true God.

At that point, it all came together for me. Jesus is alive, but I was dead in my trespasses and sins. The only hope I had was for the living Jesus to save my soul by His sheer grace. Dr. Sproul explained that this grace I desperately wanted is precisely what Jesus offers. I went from ruined to reconciled by God's grace alone!

I was newborn in the faith, and everything looked different. I had tasted a wonder that I had never known. To be sure, my understanding was dim. I had a lot of questions. But something had changed. I wanted to read the Bible. I wanted to know more about Jesus. So I sought out pastors who believed the Bible and asked them to study God's Word with me. I logged on to Ligonier's website constantly. And I continued to study the resurrection.

Now, almost seventeen years later, I have had the faith of my early twenties challenged, both in the mundane affairs of daily life and in the unsympathetic courts of academic work. I've buried loved ones and heard the spade scattering dirt on some of my dreams as well. I am a husband and father and pastor, and I've been astonished at my incapacity and inepti-tude in all three.

In a word, life—in all its beauty and knotted ugliness—has happened. But the radiance of the resurrection faith I came to believe in almost two decades ago has lost none of its luster. Indeed, as I enter middle age, it becomes more precious to me daily. Therefore, this book is not simply a detached study of evidence and exegesis. It is an act of worship by a grateful sinner who, by God's grace alone, believes that Jesus was buried but is now alive. And because of that simple yet beautiful historical fact, nothing will ever be the same for any of us.

Chapter One

A FOOL'S ERRAND?

KNOWING THE TRUTH OF THE
RESURRECTION IN AN AGE OF UNBELIEF

The American industrialist Henry Ford was known for his quick wit. One of his more memorable statements was "History is bunk." I suppose if your life's work changes the world, your witticisms get less scrutiny. In contrast to Ford's skepticism, Christianity has as one of its outstanding features its intractable commitment to history. Far from considering the past "bunk," the Bible prioritizes history. On every page, we read the evidence of the Spirit-inspired writers using careful documentation when they described historical events.

The resurrection of Christ from the dead is one of these historical events. As we will observe in later chapters, the Apostles never once imply that Jesus' resurrection was anything other than a historical fact. It was not a metaphor or a symbol. It was not a mass hallucination. Yet, despite the Bible's teaching that Jesus actually rose from the dead, skeptics insist it didn't happen.

But this kind of doubt is nothing new. In fact, the first skeptics of the resurrection were contemporaries of Jesus and the Apostles. Matthew records an agreement between the Jewish leaders and the Roman soldiers who were charged with guarding Jesus' tomb that, for a tidy sum, the guards would tell everyone that the disciples stole Jesus' body (Matt. 28:11–15). The folded graveclothes of Jesus had barely been creased when unbelief reared its cynical head.

Therefore, in this chapter, I have three goals. First, I critique the philosophical bias against the supernatural that dominates objections to the resurrection. This bias assumes certain principles that do not disprove the resurrection but reject the idea of such an event ahead of time. These assumptions, however, are fatal to this bias. Second, I look at some alternative theories put forward to explain (or better, to explain *away*) the reality of the empty tomb. Finally, I analyze and answer the arguments of two prominent scholars who are hostile to the resurrection.

THE FAITH OF DOUBT

When we moved to Mississippi, we were invited to a dinner party, which eventually turned into a supper club with dear friends. At our first meeting, we asked each other the usual get-to-know-you questions: where we were from, where we went to college, how we met our spouse, and other such pleasantries. Eventually, one of the guests asked me, "What did you study in college, Gabe?" I answered, "I did my undergraduate degree in philosophy." After a puzzled look, she responded, "Do they still have those?" I suspect many people share the viewpoint of my friend. Studying philosophy seems quaint, if not eccentric. The very mention of the word *philosophy* conjures images of long beards, obtuse arguments, and irresolvable debate.

But everyone is a philosopher, believe it or not. Philosophy is more or less asking and answering the most foundational questions of life. For example, queries like "Why am I here?" "What is the meaning of life?" "Why should I do this rather than that?" "What is true?" and "Why do LEGOs always seem to be in my path when I get up at night?" dominate philosophical speculation (especially the last one). And although we may not be professional philosophers, we are doing philosophy every time we think about matters like these. Therefore, the issue is not *whether* we will do philosophy but *how* we will do it.

Unfortunately, arguments against the resurrection display a lot of poor reasoning. In the face of overwhelming evidence that Jesus rose from the dead (evidence that we will explore later), why do so many people nevertheless reject its truth?

First and foremost, we reject God's truth because Satan has blinded our eyes (2 Cor. 4:4). Satan does this in various ways, but one common tactic is false philosophy through which the evidence is sifted. Such theorizing begins with the assumption that the human mind is competent to solve life's problems. In other words, this view rejects *at the outset* the need for divine revelation to think correctly. It rebels against the uniform testimony of the Bible that for man's mind to function as God intended, it must bow the knee to His Word. In sum, bad philosophy discards God's Word in favor of its own supremacy.

When we approach objections to Jesus' rising from the dead

on the third day, it becomes apparent they are controlled by one of these false philosophies called *naturalism* or *materialism*. We could further distinguish between *metaphysical* and *methodological* naturalism (but we'll keep things simple for the moment). Basically, naturalism teaches that nature is all there is. In this view, the God of the Bible—a tripersonal spirit who exists outside of nature—does not exist. In fact, proponents of this view argue that His existence is impossible because evidence and reason combine to prove that there is nothing beyond nature. Given this understanding of reality, the resurrection is ruled out before the evidence is even considered.

But that's the problem. It's not as though naturalism wins the ideological day because of its explanatory power or intellectual strength. Instead, it claims that it wins because of its assertion that nothing exists that cannot be sensed. That means that the philosophy of naturalism is adopted before the evidence for or against supernaturalism is examined. More than twenty years ago, Harvard biologist and committed atheist Richard Lewontin illustrated this bias when he wrote:

> Our willingness to accept scientific claims that are against common sense is the key to an understanding of the real struggle between science and the supernatural. We take the side of science *in spite* of the patent absurdity of some of its constructs, *in spite* of its failure to fulfill many of its extravagant promises of health and life, *in spite* of the tolerance of the scientific community for unsubstantiated just-so stories, because we have a prior commitment, a commitment to materialism. It is not that the methods

and institutions of science somehow compel us to accept a material explanation of the phenomenal world, but, on the contrary, that we are forced by our *a priori* adherence to material causes to create an apparatus of investigation and a set of concepts that produce material explanations, no matter how counter-intuitive, no matter how mystifying to the uninitiated. Moreover, that materialism is absolute, for we cannot allow a Divine Foot in the door.[1]

Lewontin's frank admission to the deliberate prejudice of the scientific establishment is both shocking and refreshing. It is shocking because scientists like Lewontin portray themselves as the epitome of detached, objective thought. As he said, they are not. Lewontin's admission is refreshing because it reveals what we all know implicitly. We are not as objective as we think we are; all of us are reading the evidence we come across with an implicit bias.

The last statement seems to lead us from the arms of naturalism like Lewontin's into the waiting embrace of woozy postmodernism, where truth is up for grabs and each person can have his "own" truth. But we don't have to make that choice. We have a better way. We can acknowledge that we are biased. We can grant that we are prone to distorting the evidence to meet our preconceived notions, as Lewontin admitted.

Still, these concessions don't mean that truth with a capital *T* doesn't exist. Instead of either rationalism or postmodernism, we can embrace the Bible's teaching that we are all sinners (Rom. 3:9–18), God's Word is true (John 17:17), and Jesus is the perfect incarnation of truth (John 14:6). Therefore, although we are all biased (because of sin), we can know the truth (because God has revealed it to us). In the biblical understanding, we avoid both naturalism and postmodernism.

How does this discussion pertain to the resurrection? Many of the resurrection's critics embrace the philosophy of naturalism, sometimes without confessing it (or even being aware of it). As a result, these opponents haven't actually refuted the evidence for the resurrection. They have simply read it through the lens of a different *faith*, a faith in naturalism.

Not only have these naturalists done nothing to disprove the resurrection, but they also often ignore the flaw in their own philosophy (though I'm certainly not the first to notice these weaknesses). As we will see, no one can prove the truth of naturalism. Moreover, naturalism actually undermines the very concept of truth.

First, if, as naturalism affirms, nature is all there is, then the concept of truth is meaningless. There is only what has been determined by natural selection. Stated another way, if our minds are simply our physical brains and nothing more (which is what naturalism teaches), then we have lost our minds. If every one of our thoughts is produced by the interaction of chemicals, then nothing is true or false; it simply *is*.

But if that is the case, why write books attempting to convince people that religion is false? The very act of writing a book to persuade someone assumes that minds can be changed. But minds, even assuming they exist in some sense, cannot be *changed* if they are chemically *predetermined* by some bioevolutionary mechanism. Therefore, naturalism is self-refuting from the outset. It shoots itself in the foot while claiming to run the race of intellectual freedom.

Second, if naturalism is true, morality disappears. To be clear, I am not saying that people who subscribe to naturalism are not moral. Far from it. Oftentimes, atheists can live "better" lives than professing Christians!

But whether someone *acts* morally is a separate question from whether they *should be* moral. In other words, just because you *are* moral does not mean you *should be*. The same principle from the first objection applies equally here. If nature is all there is, right and wrong do not exist. To repeat, if we are chemically predetermined to behave a certain way, then we are no longer accountable for our actions. We are just chemical machines doing what chemicals in reaction to one another do. Morality is meaningless if the naturalist is consistent.

Alex Rosenberg, professor of philosophy at Duke University, acknowledges this problem. As a committed naturalist, he believes the answers to the questions he poses would make the intellectually honest naturalist proud. When it comes to morals specifically, Rosenberg asks: "What is the difference between right and wrong, good and bad? There is no moral difference between them."[2]

This is the grim conclusion to which consistent naturalism leads. But if Rosenberg is right, then there is no point in trying to disprove the resurrection of Christ, as many critics attempt to do. After all, if morality is just an illusion, then there is no moral wrong in believing the lie the critics make the resurrection out to be. Once more, a foundational principle of naturalism is shown to be self-refuting.

The key takeaway from this discussion of naturalism as an objection to the resurrection is this: before the evidence for the resurrection is even examined, some critics who accept naturalism have already made up their minds about whatever evidence they encounter. In other words, a naturalistic explanation is preferable for these opponents to *any* supernatural explanation, no matter what evidence exists for the resurrection.

Therefore, we must recognize this position for what it is *not*. It is not rational. It is not superior to the biblical account. It is not viable, philosophically or in daily life. But we must also recognize naturalism for what it *is*. It is a faith position. It is weak intellectually. It is self-defeating. And as an attractive substitute for biblical faith, it is an utter failure.

FANCIFUL ALTERNATIVES

Much to the delight of many readers, we will now move on from philosophy to some alternative theories that skeptics have proposed to explain the empty tomb.

Broadly, we can classify the objections to Jesus' bodily resurrection into two categories: *objective* and *subjective*. When we use the term *objective*, we don't mean that such objections are objectively true. Instead, the word *objective* here simply means "external" or "able to be witnessed publicly." By contrast, when we use the word *subjective*, we refer to something experienced or observed only by the individual. In reality, this distinction is not hard and fast. But it is a useful way to distinguish various objections, so we will look at a popular example of each type.

The first alternate theory, which falls into the objective category, is called the swoon theory (ST). This is an objective theory because it purports to explain the resurrection as something other than a private hallucination or experience. The ST was popular in the nineteenth century as a means of explaining the resurrection in terms hospitable to the growing naturalism of that time. It enjoyed many advocates before being discarded in favor of other naturalistic theories.[3]

The ST teaches that Jesus did not really die on the cross but merely swooned, or fainted, only to be revived in the cool of the garden tomb. On the surface, the ST may seem reasonable. After all, history is littered with accounts of people who survive life-threatening injuries. The ST seemed especially plausible in the nineteenth century, when the evidence we have at our disposal was not available. But subsequent research has led to its almost wholesale abandonment today, as it suffers from at least three insurmountable problems.

In the first place, we have few recorded instances of any person surviving crucifixion. Indeed, most of those condemned to the Roman punishment of flogging, such as Jesus endured (John 19:1), did not even survive *that* ordeal, let alone crucifixion. The person sentenced to flogging was beaten with a gruesome instrument consisting of a whip with bits of bone and metal until his flesh was sliced to ribbons. So, this theory asks us to believe that Jesus survived flogging and *then* the horrors of the cross. With what we know today about both forms of punishment, the ST loses plausibility immediately.

Aside from the brutal torture of flogging, the cross was more catastrophic than most people understand—or want to imagine. New Testament scholar Martin Hengel has compiled an impressive array of sources from the first century to help us understand something of the trauma of crucifixion. The testimony of these ancient eyewitnesses bears witness to the impossibility of the ST.

To cite just one example, Hengel references the words of the great Roman orator Seneca, who described what it was like to see a crucifixion: "Can anyone be found who would prefer wasting away in pain dying limb by limb, or letting out his life drop by drop, rather than expiring once for all? Can any man be found willing to be fastened to the accursed tree, long sickly, already deformed, swelling with ugly weals on shoulders and chest, and drawing the breath of life amid long drawn-out agony?"[4] What Seneca meant was that he could not imagine a more dreadful way to die.

The cross's extreme suffering was by design. Rome employed it to deter any and all criminal action. Before the cross was totally transformed by Jesus' death into a symbol of Christianity, its message was simple, brutal, and effective: "Do not mess with Rome." It was the ancient equivalent of the electric chair.

In the second place, the ST asks us to believe (with a straight face) that not only did Jesus survive flogging and the crucifixion, but He also managed to roll away, in a half-dead condition, a stone that weighed thousands of pounds. But that would be impossible for even a healthy man to accomplish!

Third, the ST requires us to further believe that, having rolled the stone away, Jesus then single-handedly defeated the Roman equivalent of a Navy SEAL team or convinced them to let Him go. These soldiers' survival depended on guarding the tomb, for Roman soldiers took their own lives or were killed if they failed in their assignment. So they would have had zero motivation to release Jesus even if He had managed to roll the stone away.

In light of these problems, the ST reveals itself as a desperate attempt to avoid the biblical account of the resurrection. Again, it is not so much an explanation as it is an attempt to explain *away* the evidence of Jesus' resurrection in naturalistic terms.

A far more popular view is what is known as the hallucination theory (HT). It comes in many forms; resurrection expert Gary Habermas has written a very helpful article summarizing them.[5] More recently, Michael Licona's exhaustive treatment of the various naturalistic proposals, including the HT, shows them all to be wanting.[6] Essentially, the HT claims that Jesus' postmortem appearances were either individual or collective hallucinations. As outlined above, these various alternatives could be classified as *subjective*.

As with the ST, the HT suffers from numerous flaws, which Habermas explains. We'll focus on three difficulties with this theory. First, hallucinations are *private* experiences. A group hallucination—such as that mentioned in 1 Corinthians 15:6, where Jesus appeared to some five hundred people—is nearly impossible.

Second, Jesus' postresurrection appearances varied widely in terms of location and time. That the known eyewitnesses would have had the same hallucination over many different places and times is not plausible.

Third, if the Apostles were having hallucinations about Jesus' being alive and were preaching this bothersome doctrine, all the officials in Jerusalem had to do was produce the body to put such delusions to rest (no pun intended).[7] Once again, this theory cannot explain the facts we know about the resurrection.

Whether objective or subjective, alternatives to the biblical record of Jesus' resurrection all lack credibility. To illustrate this point further, we will next look at some authors who hold to these substitute theories. In each case, their objections to the resurrection cannot stand up to investigation.

FIERCE OBJECTIONS

Our first critic is the retired Episcopalian bishop John Shelby Spong. He is a noted popularizer of liberal theology over the past two decades. Like most of those in church history who deny cardinal tenets of the Christian faith, Spong is convinced that Christianity is in danger of becoming extinct. Therefore, for Christianity to survive in the modern age, it must, to quote the title of one of his books, "change or die."

One of the bishop's proposed changes is a full-scale denial of the resurrection of Christ. He makes this very clear when he writes: "Angels who descend in earthquakes, speak, and disappear . . . empty tombs . . . these are legends all. Sacred legends, I might add, but legends nonetheless."[8]

In place of the bodily resurrection of Jesus, Spong proposes a naturalistic explanation, a species of the HT that Habermas calls the illumination theory. This is not to say that Spong is an atheist like Richard Lewontin. Rather, his explanations of the resurrection simply evidence a subterranean commitment to a variety of naturalism.

In his book *Resurrection: Myth or Fact?*, Spong proposes the following scenario: discouraged by Jesus' violent death and the seeming end of the promised coming kingdom, Peter and the other Apostles went back to their daily lives. But Peter couldn't forget Jesus.

After grieving and processing Jesus' death, Peter returned to his work as a fisherman, Spong theorizes. "On a hunch, Simon changed nets from one side of the boat to the other, with strikingly good results."[9] This is Spong's naturalistic explanation for the miraculous catch of fish recorded in John 21:4–7. Peter's experience led him to believe that Jesus was alive. Spong explains: "Suddenly it all came together for Simon. The crucifixion was not punitive, it was intentional. . . . It would be fair to say that in that moment Simon felt resurrected. The clouds of grief, confusion, and depression vanished from his mind, and in that moment he knew that Jesus was part of the very essence of God, and at that moment Simon saw Jesus alive."[10]

Not *actually* alive, of course. Spong has already told us that a Jesus who was resurrected bodily is nothing more than pious legend. No, according to Spong, Peter *felt* Jesus to be alive and went on to evangelize *as if* Jesus were alive.

Notice what Spong has done. First, he has assumed that certain parts of the New Testament record (such as breakfast on the beach and Peter's catching fish) are true. But that assumption militates against the skepticism he advocated earlier in the same book. In chapter 3, Spong argues at length that because God's Word is such an "unsteady ship" (his words), we must seek the truth *behind* the words of the text.[11] In other words, the biblical text is unreliable.

Despite the unreliable nature of Scripture, Spong has nevertheless treated some of it as true. In reality, he has taken the liberty to choose which parts of the biblical account are reliable and has then explained them in terms of naturalism. From the perspective of logical consistency, Spong's exercise is viciously circular. He has assumed what he sets out to prove.

Second, Spong's far-fetched explanation of the resurrection ignores much of the specific evidence that the New Testament is trustworthy. Textual criticism is the discipline that studies the development of the biblical text in its original languages to determine the most accurate reading for translations. One scholar summarizes the evidence this way: "It is reassuring at the end to find that the general result of all these discoveries and all this study is to strengthen the proof of the authenticity of the Scriptures, and our conviction that we have in our hands, in substantial integrity, the veritable word of God."[12] In other words, the results of textual criticism reinforce our conviction that we can trust our Bibles.

A third problem with Spong's work is his fallacious appeal to authority. He laments: "If the resurrection of Jesus cannot be believed except by assenting to the fantastic descriptions included in the gospels, then Christianity is doomed. For that view of the resurrection is not believable. . . . If that were a requirement of belief as a Christian, then I would sadly leave my house of faith. With me in that exodus would be every ranking New Testament scholar in the world."[13] Spong then goes on to list a host of scholars who also reject Christ's resurrection.

His list of "ranking scholars" does not, however, disprove the resurrection. Instead, it exemplifies the informal logical fallacy *argumentum ad populum*, or appeal to the majority. This is the mistaken notion that because a majority of people believe something, it must be true.

I like to call this "Your Mother's Favorite Fallacy." Most of us can remember wanting to go with friends to a concert or movie that was probably not the best thing for us to see. When denied the opportunity, we argued, "But Mom, everyone is going!" The response was as swift as it was predictable. "Just because everyone else is doing it doesn't make it right." Case closed, fun denied!

Mom's reasoning is irrefutable, though, as a closer examination of Spong's appeal to the "majority" of New Testament scholars demonstrates. He overlooks the impressive list one could easily compile of scholars with similar accomplishments who argue that the resurrection did in fact happen as the New Testament records.

Therefore, the question is once again not about which side is more scholarly; both sides have doctorates and accolades. Nor will the question be settled by an appeal to the majority of scholars, for majorities can be wrong and scholars read evidence differently. Ultimately, Spong's attempt to disprove the resurrection by an appeal to the majority of experts is little more than a hollow claim that is exposed with an appeal to Mom's reasoning.

Having addressed Spong's claims, we move on to those of Dr. Bart Ehrman, a prolific author, an agnostic, and an expert in textual criticism. His books are regular best sellers on the *New York Times* list. In addition, he's built something of a cottage industry around his work, the central focus of which is to cast doubt on the reliability of the New Testament. Since he believes the New Testament was changed on purpose, it is a short step for him to deny the resurrection, which is exactly what he did in a debate with Christian apologist William Lane Craig.

Ehrman's arguments against the resurrection are straightforward. First, as mentioned above, he believes that the New Testament manuscripts were changed during their transmission by the scribes who copied them, to the point that the original reports of what actually happened are lost forever. Here's how he articulates his position:

[The Gospels] are not historically reliable accounts. The authors were not eyewitnesses; they're Greek-speaking Christians living 35 to 65 years after the events they narrate. The accounts that they narrate are based on oral traditions that have been in circulation for decades. Year after year Christians trying to convert others told them stories to convince them that Jesus was raised from the dead. These writers are telling stories, then, that Christians have been telling all these years. Many stories were invented, and most of the stories were changed.[14]

Because Ehrman considers this difficulty insurmountable, we will start with it. Ehrman argues that events recorded by those who knew the eyewitnesses should be rejected out of hand. The first problem with this view is that carried to its logical end, all of ancient history becomes unreliable.

Moreover, it's pure speculation to say that the eyewitnesses changed their testimony. The evidence indicates quite the contrary. The New Testament text was copied largely by scribes who were not from Israel and would not have had firsthand knowledge of distinctly Jewish customs. Yet the New Testament abounds in "local knowledge," from geography to town names to Jewish traditions. Textual critic and New Testament scholar Peter Williams explains: "Our Gospel manuscripts mostly come from outside of Palestine, from countries such as Egypt, Italy, Greece, or Turkey. We can hardly suppose that scribes in these countries were responsible for introducing accurate Palestinian cultural knowledge into the Gospels."[15] If anything, the more we discover, the more the New Testament proves itself to be one of the most trustworthy ancient documents that we possess today.

The sheer number of New Testament manuscripts is a major reason why we can establish its dependability. For example, it is not fashionable to argue that Plato's major works are in doubt. Yet the manuscript data for his writings is small, limited to a handful of late copies. In stark contrast, we have *thousands* of early copies of the New Testament. It is far and away the most well-attested ancient document there is, and there is a remarkable amount of agreement between these manuscripts. This means that Ehrman's contention that evidence of textual corruption disproves the resurrection is false.

Following from his argument that the Gospels are unreliable historical accounts, Ehrman claims that a miracle like the resurrection is an unreasonable explanation for what happened to Jesus' body. Instead, the resurrection is part and parcel of the fabricated stories that accrued after Christianity came on the scene.

Instead of a bald antisupernaturalism like we witnessed with Spong, Ehrman strikes a more agnostic pose toward the resurrection of Christ. "I'm not saying it didn't happen; but if it did happen, it would be a miracle. . . . I wish we could establish miracles, but we can't. It's no one's fault. It's simply that the canons of historical research do not allow for the possibility of establishing as probable the least probable of all occurrences."[16] The last sentence is key to understanding Ehrman's position. According to him, historical research only deals with the probable and a miracle like the resurrection is the least probable of all occurrences. Therefore, it is highly unlikely that it happened.

Despite his claims to a cool, detached agnosticism, Ehrman's view of miracles and probability betray a firm naturalistic understanding of both. He asks: "What are miracles? Miracles are not impossible. . . . They violate the way nature naturally works. They are so highly improbable, their probability is infinitesimally remote, that we call them miracles."[17] Now, William Lane Craig, the Christian who debated Ehrman, is a skilled philosopher who used probability theory in his reply to Ehrman. Craig's reply made it painfully obvious that Ehrman was out of his league when it came to probability theory. Craig demonstrated, in exhaustive detail (replete with mathematical equations), that Ehrman's assertion that miracles are improbable is mistaken.

This is not the place to work through Craig's reply in an in-depth manner. To keep things simple, let's go back to our earlier discussion about philosophy. Even before he considers the evidence for the resurrection, Ehrman's understanding of miracles raises some significant philosophical issues.

Notice his assumption that miracles violate the way nature works. But this simply begs the question in favor of his view. In other words, he defines miracles in a way that excludes the miraculous. Moreover, Ehrman can never prove that miracles violate the laws of nature. He has not observed all of nature to make such a sweeping claim. Indeed, no one has. Nor *could* anyone.

Therefore, Ehrman's claim that miracles violate the laws of nature amounts to a faith position that is inconsistent with itself and with the actual evidence. As R.C. Sproul, John Gerstner, and Arthur Lindsley observe: "The biblical miracles need to be considered on their own merits. Their impossibility, or even improbability, has never been demonstrated. We have positive evidence for their occurrence. The reasonable person will believe that they occurred as recorded."[18]

The views of Spong and Ehrman offer us a snapshot of resurrection skepticism. To be sure, others have offered even more sophisticated objections, but believing scholars have answered them well. As a result, objections of this variety do not disprove the resurrection.

CONCLUSION

In this chapter, we have examined the faulty philosophical basis from which the critics of the resurrection work. We have seen that the alternative theories for the resurrection cannot stand up to careful scrutiny. And we dissected the objections of two accomplished scholars who object to the resurrection and discovered that their claims are little more than assertions that lack careful arguments. But our goal in this book is not just to criticize; it is also to construct. Therefore, in the next chapter, we will argue why the resurrection is true.

Chapter Two

FOR SURE

THE EVIDENCE
FOR THE RESURRECTION

Mark Twain, one of America's greatest writers, did not hold any kind of religious belief in high regard. His definition of faith was as simple as it was biting: "Faith is believing what you know ain't so."

Although perhaps expressed with less wit, Twain's sentiment is still prevalent today. This view of faith, however, reveals a persistent misunderstanding of what faith is and what it is not. Unpacking those differences would take us beyond the scope of this book. For now, we can simply note that the God of the Bible never calls for "blind" faith like that which Twain scorned. Just the opposite, in fact. God gives us His Word to trust, and He acts in the history He decreed (Heb. 11:1). If one of the prophets or Apostles heard Twain's witty slogan, he might reply, "Faith is believing what everybody knows is so" (see Rom. 1:18–32).

Whatever the disagreement about the nature of faith, people see little controversy about facts. Facts are public; faith is private. Facts are certain; faith is subjective. So, is the resurrection faith or fact?

I think that's the wrong way to frame the issue. The Scriptures don't force us to choose between faith and facts. Instead, the Bible presents the resurrection as accepted by a *certain kind* of faith while teaching that it is a *certain kind* of fact.

While there is a lot of evidence that demonstrates the historical reality that Jesus rose from the dead, I've organized some of the main arguments under four headings (complete with a lame acronym!). The resurrection of Christ is *T.R.U.E.* for the following four reasons: it explains the *transformation* of the disciples, it is *rationally* satisfying, it makes our world *understandable*, and it *explains* all the evidence. Taken together, these lines of evidence demonstrate that the resurrection is not a leap of faith (in Twain's sense of the term) but a well-established fact.

IT EXPLAINS THE TRANSFORMATION OF THE DISCIPLES

We can make many compelling arguments for the truthfulness of the Bible, but here is one that is often overlooked. The Scriptures record, without flinching and often in heart-wrenching detail, the massive flaws of its heroes. No attempt is made to downplay their failures. In the Old Testament alone, from Abraham's lying about Sarah's identity (Gen. 20:9) to King David's adulterous, murderous ways (2 Sam. 11:1–26), the "best" of the Bible are the worst by even the "moral" standards of people who wouldn't profess to be Christians.

We might expect the situation to improve when we come to the New Testament. After all, the twelve Apostles had Jesus—God in the flesh—as their leader and teacher. Without a doubt, they must have done better than their Old Testament forerunners.

But, of course, they didn't. They misunderstood Jesus all the time. They were full of unbelief. By all accounts, they were comprehensive failures, full of sin, like their Old Testament predecessors—and like us.

When confronted with the evidence of Jesus' deity after He fed the multitudes, they worried about where their next meal was coming from (Matt. 16:5–12). Having witnessed Jesus heal the sick and cast out demons for years, they still thought the kingdom of heaven was about them (Mark 9:50; Luke 22:24). On the night of Jesus' arrest, they couldn't even stay awake to pray for the One who had prayed for them daily (Matt. 26:36–46). Ultimately, when our Lord needed them the most, they fled and hid themselves like cowards (Matt. 26:56). All told, when we meet the twelve Apostles in the New Testament, we are introduced to a group whose prospects seem very limited indeed. Certainly, they are not those with whom we would entrust the most important message in history!

In a strange way, I find the failure of the disciples comforting, for I can identify with them. I often let Jesus down, but He never gives up on me. Nonetheless, the disciples' repeated inability to grasp the message and the miracles of Jesus does more than elicit our sympathy. Their failure sets the stage for one of the greatest turnarounds in history.

We have dear friends whose son worked for the New England Patriots. I was raised a die-hard Dallas Cowboys fan (which, in recent years, has prepared me to handle disappointment well!), so I never cheered for the Pats. But because of my friend's connection with the Patriots, I began to pay attention to them. Their 2017 Super Bowl comeback was one of the most memorable in NFL history. Though the Patriots were down 21-3 to the Atlanta Falcons at the half, Tom Brady guided New England to a 34-28 overtime win. If nothing else, it was a riveting story, because we all love a good comeback.

As big as the stage was for Brady's come-from-behind win, it is still trivial compared to what happened to the disciples. Their "comeback" ranks as the greatest about-face in history. Before seeing Jesus after His resurrection, they were huddled away for fear of the authorities (John 20:19). But when they saw the risen Lord, everything changed.

Peter exemplified this transformation. In the garden of Gethsemane, he promised that he would never leave Jesus' side (Matt. 26:33). Yet, a short while later, he was brought to the point of renouncing Jesus with curses by—wait for it—a young servant (Luke 22:56). Not one of the many fearsome warriors guarding Pilate that night. Not even by a grown man. Peter's downfall came at the hands of a teenager.

In spite of his failure that night, Peter became the mighty preacher of Pentecost. The other disciples followed suit, as we'll see in chapter 4. Their transformation was as complete as their failure.

Here's the point. The disciples' transformation is inexplicable if Jesus did not rise bodily from the dead. They had every possible social deterrent for believing the resurrection. They would lose their sense of community by being cast out of the synagogue (John 9:22). They would lose their families. They would even face death (Acts 5:33). Yet they continued preaching and teaching the resurrection (Acts 5:41). Why? Because normal people do not risk everything for a lie.

Now, that's a broad principle. So let's narrow it down. We can all imagine counterexamples to the claim that people don't die for something they know isn't true. Skeptics argue: "Lots of people die for false causes. After all, as a Christian, you believe that Islam is not true. Yet plenty of people give their lives willingly for this supposed delusion all the time." There are a few problems with this response.

First, Christians can show that Islam is not true. Second, this objection assumes that all religions are the same. Third, it further assumes that giving one's life in service of one religion is the same as the early disciples' being willing to give up their lives in defense of the resurrection.

The twelve Apostles were dying not just for *principles* (as is the case with many other religious martyrdoms) but for a *person*. According to their message, this person is the God-man, and He is alive. As one scholar explains, "If the original disciples had not believed that they had seen the resurrected Jesus, their firm commitment to the Christian faith after the death of their leader is not easily explained."[1]

The previous chapter catalogued the naturalistic presuppositions that drive critics to reinterpret the resurrection. The same assumptions are in play in the objections to the disciples' transformation. Those who make these objections assume that nature is all there is and then try to explain the disciples' change in terms of nature alone.

But, once again, the alternative scenarios don't withstand

careful analysis. The disciples' change from a cowardly band to bold preachers can only be explained by this simple fact: They were transformed because what they were proclaiming happened. Jesus was raised from the dead.

IT IS RATIONALLY SATISFYING

The second letter of our acronym states that the biblical account of the resurrection offers a rationally satisfying assessment of the evidence. Stating the matter this way may seem counterintuitive. After all, we live in a scientific age. To paraphrase Spong's remarks from the last chapter, the notion that a corpse has risen from the grave seems to be a sacred legend. But as we saw in the first chapter, alternative explanations to the Bible's account of the resurrection have all been found wanting.

A delightful scene in C.S. Lewis' classic *The Lion, the Witch and the Wardrobe* illustrates my point. Lucy reports to her older siblings, Peter, Edmund, and Susan, that she was transported to another realm via a magic wardrobe. They are incredulous, to the point of worrying about her sanity. So, they take her to see the eccentric old professor in whose home they are staying.

He listens to their complaints and then responds with some incredulity of his own. "'Logic!' said the Professor half to himself. 'Why don't they teach logic at these schools! There are only three possibilities. Either your sister is telling lies, or she is mad, or she is telling the truth. You know she doesn't lie, and it is obvious that she is not mad.'"[2] The professor's conclusion is inescapable. If the witness is sane (which Lucy was) and the other alternatives fail to explain the evidence at hand (which they did), then it is rational to believe the eyewitness's account.

Similarly, when we turn to the New Testament and examine the accounts of Jesus' resurrection, no evidence suggests that the hundreds of eyewitnesses were not sane. They would go on to offer the world some of the highest moral teaching it has ever heard. Lying witnesses don't do that. Furthermore, the alternatives to the New Testament record fail to explain the evidence. Therefore, the only rational conclusion is to believe their claim that Jesus rose from the dead.

Lurking beneath the denial of the resurrection as an irrational legend is the assumption that miracles are impossible or, at best, highly improbable. As we observed in the last chapter, this is Bart Ehrman's position. It is based on a mistaken view of God and His dealings with creation.

What unbelief categorizes as "natural laws," the Scriptures call "ordinary providence." For example, ordinarily a falling object goes down due to the law of gravity. This law, along with a host of other principles, epitomizes God's ordinary providence in this world.

The Bible claims that the way the world works in everyday life is a result of God's upholding certain norms through His moment-by-moment providence (see Heb. 1:3). Likewise, the fact that we even have natural laws that apply across time and space (gravity doesn't change when you go from America on Monday to Europe on Wednesday!) indicates that something far more than a mechanized natural process is at work.

Even so, since at least the time of Scottish philosopher David Hume in the eighteenth century, scholars have insisted that miracles violate natural laws. Yet again, this is an assumption that cannot be proven. How could anyone test the laws of nature in every time, place, and situation to know that they apply in the same way? It can't be done. Therefore, we must *assume* these laws in order to do science, medicine, and so on.

As a result, we return to a familiar question: Which worldview can underwrite these kinds of assumptions? Only Christianity can do so, as we have seen. In the biblical world- view, God determines what we call laws of nature. Because God is dependable and has promised to govern the world in an orderly fashion (Gen. 8:22), we can trust nature to work in a certain way.

Delving a bit deeper, we see that critics enamored of a godless conception of natural law make the mistake of exalting laws over God. They are engaging in a form of idolatry, even if it is cloaked in the garb of nonreligious, "rational" skepticism. They assume that natural laws, not God, are ultimate. But here's the irony. Natural laws cannot explain natural laws or prove natural laws. Ultimately, the argument that miracles are impossible because they violate natural laws is merely circular.

What does all this have to do with the resurrection as a rationally satisfying explanation of the evidence? It highlights the fact that only a worldview where the resurrection is possible—the biblical worldview—makes rationality, well, *rational*. If we opt for an understanding of the world where God cannot intervene and nature is a closed system, we don't just exclude God. We make *rationality* impossible. Or, to restate the argument from the last chapter, if nature is all there is, then striving after rationality is useless.

IT MAKES OUR WORLD UNDERSTANDABLE

The third line of evidence follows from the second. The resurrection of Christ makes our world understandable. That is, a universe in which God keeps His promises by raising Christ from the dead helps us order our lives. Stated in different terms, the world is not the place contemporary opinion makers tell us it is. Our lives are not a chaotic, meaningless combination of random experiences. We are not left to ourselves in search of some fleeting value for our otherwise miserable existence.

One of the ways we know a certain conception of reality is true or false is its ability to make sense of the world around us. For example, some forms of paganism argue that headaches are caused by evil spirits. If we want to relieve the suffering, we need to get rid of the evil spirit through some ritual or ceremony. But neither the diagnosis nor the cure explains headaches as well as modern medicine does. In this case, what we believe about reality is obvious, and painfully so (pardon the bad pun).

The resurrection and the biblical worldview of which it is a part make sense of the world around us in a way that no other worldview can. Despite the Bible's explanatory power, most people have embraced a different worldview, which I will call moderate nihilism. *Nihilism* comes from the Latin word *nihil*, which means "nothing." This philosophy teaches that reality is ultimately without meaning.

Carried to its logical conclusions, *full-blown* nihilism would drive most people to insanity. But we are, mercifully, never consistent with our principles. As a result, the default setting for many people today is what I call *moderate* nihilism.

More than 150 years ago, Henry David Thoreau, in his defining work *Walden*, captured the essence of moderate nihilism when he wrote, "The mass of men lead lives of quiet desperation." The culture around us tends to view life as a bleak winter landscape, punctuated by a few momentary rays of sunlight, before the gloom of an everlasting night engulfs all that we know.

Where does this quiet desperation, this moderate nihilism, come from? Of course, the answer is complex, but at least two main causes point to an explanation. First, the rise of Darwinism has had a profound influence on modern culture. Second, the loss of confidence in the Bible's truthfulness contributes to the nihilistic haze that hangs over our lives.

We can feel the influence of Darwinism everywhere, almost imperceptively—from the local museum's exhibits, to the advertisements we see, to the institutions where our children are educated. How does the rise of Darwinism lead to moderate nihilism?

According to Charles Darwin's philosophy, what matters is survival, not truth. It teaches that, at bottom, reality is a giant accident. Time plus chance leads to Beethoven's *Emperor* Concerto. Our lives can have no real meaning, for meaning depends on truth.

That's not to say that Darwin didn't believe his system was true. He believed passionately that his ideas were true! But that is a far cry from saying he believed (or his views *allowed* him to believe) in truth in any transcendent sense.

If one supposes that all is ultimately nothing but a chance arrangement of matter and energy, that core belief will have a profound influence in one's life. Work is futile. Love is momentary. Art is bizarre. Beauty is pointless. As R.C. Sproul put it, ideas have consequences, and that is true of Darwinism as much as for any other philosophy.

Recent architecture illustrates the effect of moderate nihilism. Most of the buildings constructed in the past sixty or so years are concrete juggernauts, with little to no structural beauty. They proclaim, with concrete and steel, what moderate nihilism believes in the abstract. They are useful but they are ugly. In their silence, they send a clear message into our daily horizons. Life is hard, life is bleak, and we have no hope.

No arches draw the wandering eye to the "starry heavens above," to borrow Immanuel Kant's language. Instead, harsh, jagged superstructures mar our cities. They stand in frowning contrast to the buildings of a bygone era. These bear eloquent testimony to a time when the ordinary could still be beautiful. Today, such buildings seem as quaint as the opening scene in *Our Town*.

Sadly, Darwin lived out the implications of his philosophy for art, beauty, and the like. Later in his life, he wrote:

> Up to the age of thirty, or beyond it, poetry of many kinds, such as the works of Milton, Gray, Byron, Wordsworth, Coleridge, and Shelley, gave me great pleasure, and even as a schoolboy I took intense delight in Shakespeare, especially in the historical plays. I have also said that formerly pictures gave me considerable, and music very great delight. But now for many years I cannot endure to read a line of poetry: I have tried lately to read Shakespeare, and found it so intolerably dull that it nauseated me. . . . My mind seems to have become a kind of machine for grinding general laws out of large collections of facts.[3]

A good indicator that our thinking has gone astray is when something as intrinsically delightful as poetry or music makes us reach for the Pepto.

Darwin's ideas affect the modern world far more than we might imagine, resulting in hollow souls and fractured lives. The quiet desperation described by Thoreau has morphed into an all-encompassing despair. Many people believe that this life, with all its pain, suffering, and ugliness, is the sum total of reality. With such a grim view of the ordinary, is it any wonder that we long for something more than superficial relationships, mundane commutes, and momentary pleasure? The ascent of man championed by Darwin has turned out to be the *descent* of man into the yawning chasm of gnawing despondency.

There is a second reason for the rise of moderate nihilism, and that is the loss of faith in the Bible's truthfulness. Once Darwinism gained the intellectual field, what had been a steady trickle of biblical criticism turned into a flood of unbelief. Most of those who denied the Bible's truthfulness did so because of Darwin's teachings. For these academics, "true science" was synonymous with Darwinism. Therefore, the Bible may contain useful moral guidance, but it certainly isn't true in the scientific sense.

The newfound optimism stemming from Darwin's philosophy held out the promise of a world that had matured beyond superstitious religious bigotry. Severed from a benighted past in which God ruled the world and spoke to people, mankind would finally realize his full potential.

But this optimism, so characteristic of the late nineteenth and early twentieth centuries, was obliterated by an economic depression and two world wars. Regimes that embraced Darwin's ideas (such as those of Adolf Hitler and Joseph Stalin) sent massive numbers of the world's population to early graves or grueling imprisonment. When the dust from these cultural upheavals settled, people faced a brave new world. And it terrified them.

But where could they turn for hope? The Bible had been discarded as contemptible fiction. Modernism's promises were bankrupt. Moderate nihilism crept in as the post–World War II generation came of age.

While churches were full of people during the 1950s and '60s in America, many of those churches were devoid of any authoritative biblical preaching and teaching. The next generation abandoned the churches their parents and grandparents had built. They searched for hope and found glad-handing ministers who smiled and gave them nothing but moral stories. They looked for something beyond a world of splintered dreams and were answered with the pleasant impoverishment of educated unbelief in their pulpits.

Today, the baby boomers' children and grandchildren are still searching for something beyond the despair of the present. Moderate nihilism continues to grip the West. But this result is not surprising.

When we have told generations that the Bible is unbelievable, are we surprised that people listened and lived accordingly? Should we really be shocked that a world shorn of hope and overwhelmed by violence flees to internet pornography for escape? Is it any wonder that people who have been told that their bodies are nothing but matter and energy are killing children in their wombs at unprecedented levels? Are we really taken aback that pills seem preferable to the drudgery of a life in which poetry causes us to vomit? To return to Sproul's book title mentioned above, ideas have consequences. The consequences of moderate nihilism have been nothing but misery for the human race.

As an aside, we should also be clear that nothing I have written suggests that Christians should be afraid of science. Nor should Christians be "anti-science." True science is, to borrow Johannes Kepler's immortal phrase, "thinking God's thoughts after him." Of all people, Christians should embrace science for what it is: the study of God's revelation of Himself in the natural world.

What Christians must and should oppose is the godless *mis*use of science in service of philosophies that inhibit human flourishing. Without a doubt, Darwin himself would not have supported some of the results that have followed from his ideas. Still, the unintended results of his theory have been disastrous. For this reason, Christians should be contributing to the rich storehouse of scientific knowledge while at the same time resisting all efforts to weaponize science in service of anti-Christian philosophies.

The resurrection of Jesus makes better sense of our world than its chief rival, moderate nihilism. At a time when people are desperate to understand the confused age in which we live, the Bible offers us a picture of the world that explains why there is so much suffering, evil, and sin. But it doesn't stop there. It also offers us the hope of new and better life. Jesus' return from the grave seals this hope. This is why God's Word says that this kind of hope "does not put us to shame" (Rom. 5:5).

As we have seen, critics of the resurrection often paint themselves as the champions of rational thought. But if they reject the resurrection and the worldview that makes it possible, they have committed themselves to any number of irrational philosophies, not the least of which is moderate nihilism. Therefore, a Christian is more than justified in asking the critic, "What could be more rational than taking God at His word?" When we do, the brightness of resurrection life dissipates the nihilistic gloom that engulfs our lives.

Therefore, one of the ways we know that the resurrection is true is that it is rationally satisfying. Truth be told, the very fact that we seek a satisfying explanation for the events in our lives reminds us that we bear the image of a God who loves order and reason. Viewed from this perspective, it is only natural that we who are made in His image would seek rational explanations for what happens around us. The resurrection makes our world understandable.

IT EXPLAINS ALL THE EVIDENCE

The final letter of our acronym states that the resurrection of Jesus is true because it explains all the available evidence. Other theories can explain *aspects* of the New Testament and extrabiblical historical accounts of Jesus' rising from the dead. They can account for *some* of the facts. But they can't make sense of the *whole picture*. In other words, the problem with the other theories is not so much what they *can* explain about the resurrection but what they *can't* explain.

Put another way, one of the means we use to assess the correctness of a theory when we are seeking to explain a given set of facts is to determine whether that theory best accounts for the evidence we have. This is not to say a true theory will have no anomalies. There will always be some facts that seem to contradict the theory. But it is rational, when choosing among theories, to select the one that explains the most facts with the fewest inconsistencies.

When it comes to the resurrection, the New Testament record of Christ's resurrection is the only theory that fits this criterion. It accounts for everything we know about why the tomb was empty on the third day. It doesn't sacrifice inconvenient facts on the altar of a treasured theory, as the alternatives do.

As we have seen, the Bible's account of the resurrection explains why the disciples were so signally transformed. And, for example, it also details why Paul was convinced that he had met Jesus. It vindicates why the Christian church went from a despised sect of Judaism in the first century to the world's largest religion in the twenty-first century.

Two qualifications merit consideration at this point. First, when we say the biblical record explains all the evidence, we are not saying that the New Testament answers all our questions about the resurrection. In fact, there are many unanswered questions. How did Jesus' resurrection body disappear, seemingly at will (Luke 24:31)? What will the age of our bodies be when we're resurrected? Why didn't Jesus appear to more people after the resurrection?

The Bible has little to say on these and a host of related questions. But just because the Bible doesn't answer them is no reason to doubt the biblical record. To state the obvious, all it means is that the Bible doesn't answer all our questions.

The fact that we do not have the answers to all our questions should not be a hindrance to faith. More particularly, these kinds of problems reveal whether we are worshiping the living and true God or a god of our own making. The biblical God does things we don't understand (Isa. 55:8–9). The biblical God does not owe us—His fallen, sinful, rebellious creatures—an explanation for all He does (Rom. 9:20). If, after careful study of the Bible, we still find ourselves with a perplexing difficulty, the solution is not to doubt the truthfulness of the Bible. On the contrary, our ignorance is a call to worship the One who "does all that he pleases" (Ps. 115:3) and declares "the end from the beginning" (Isa. 46:10).

Second, if the resurrection is true, why don't more people believe it? Or, to ask it a different way, if the evidence for the resurrection is as clear as we have made it out to be, then why isn't everyone convinced? As we observed in the previous chapter, sin blinds us from accepting the truth. It bears repeating that unbelief involves an element of spiritual warfare.

We must never think that the debate about the resurrection is simply a debate about a historical event (or its lack of historicity). It is never just an intellectual exercise. It is, at its core, a spiritual question (2 Cor. 4:4).

In light of this tragic situation, Christians should be humbled by God's astonishing grace. We have believed not because we're smarter or because we grasped the obvious on our own but only because God opened our eyes to see His truth (see Acts 26:18).

But Christians should not only be humbled; we should also be emboldened. Confident that God will use the truth of His Word to turn people to Himself, we can have ultimate confidence in our beliefs. The faith that believes the resurrection is not misplaced. It is grounded on the truth of God's Word as the only plausible explanation of why the tomb is empty. We will explore this scriptural evidence further in the next two chapters.

EVIDENCE OUTSIDE THE BIBLE?

Is there evidence for the resurrection of Jesus outside the biblical books? The answer is yes. We will look briefly at two key texts that mention the resurrection of Christ.

In the eyes of most people, Tacitus (AD 56–120) was the greatest Roman historian.[4] When writing in 116 about the burning of Rome in 64, he mentions Jesus. Commenting on Nero's cruelty toward Christians after the fire, Tacitus writes: "Nero created scapegoats and subjected to the most refined tortures those whom the common people called 'Christians,' [a group] hated for their abominable crimes. Their name comes from Christ, who, during the reign of Tiberius, had been executed by the procurator Pontius Pilate. Suppressed for the moment, the deadly superstition broke out again, not only in Judea, the land which originated this evil, but also in the city of Rome."[5]

These remarks offer us a glimpse of how early non-Christians perceived the new religion. To put it mildly, their opinion was not flattering. But if we overlook the negative rhetoric, Tacitus' writing sheds light on the truth of the resurrection, which was certainly not his intention!

First, he mentions Tiberius and Pontius Pilate by name in connection with Jesus. So, less than a century after the crucifixion and resurrection of Jesus, a highly respected non-Christian historian tells us that Jesus was a historical figure. Moreover, in doing so, he corroborates names that New Testament writers also noted (see Luke 3:1; Acts 4:27).

Second, he refers to the "deadly superstition." What is he talking about? It can only be the resurrection. The fact that Tacitus mentions this belief shows how fast the resurrection had become a cardinal tenet of the Christian faith. Of course, Tacitus doesn't believe it (hence his term "superstition").

But that is unimportant. What concerns us is that Christians were known from the earliest times as those who believed that

Jesus had been raised from the dead. For these ancient believers, it was a nonnegotiable article of faith.

Third, Tacitus' account shows us how quickly belief in Jesus' resurrection had spread. Nero's persecutions failed to snuff out the infant religion. It would have been much to Nero's horror, no doubt, that the resurrection faith was so widespread that by the time Tacitus wrote, it was well known in Rome.

It continued to explode. Nero would have never imagined that less than 250 years from the time that he was burning Christians alive, the emperor Constantine would pronounce Rome a Christian empire (c. 312).

Therefore, Tacitus provides us with an early non-Christian substantiation of the New Testament teaching about Jesus. In addition, there are other early sources that mention the resurrection of Jesus.

In the second place, we will look at the writings of the early church father Ignatius of Antioch, who lived from AD 35 to 107. We have seven letters he wrote as he was transported to Rome to face martyrdom.

He states his belief in the resurrection of Jesus in plain terms: "For I know and believe that after the resurrection he was in the flesh. And when he came to the people around Peter, he said to them, 'Take, handle me and see, that I am not a bodiless phantom.'"[6]

Ignatius is best remembered for combatting a heresy known as Docetism.[7] This sect taught that Jesus only *seemed* to be a real person but was not, in fact (the name Docetism comes from the Greek verb that means "to appear"). Ignatius battled this heresy by reminding his readers that Jesus was raised *bodily* from the grave.

He appeared *bodily* to His disciples (more on this in chapter 4). Our Lord did not merely *seem* to be a man. He took on true flesh and blood and was raised from the dead in a glorified body.

These two early sources confirm what we have witnessed so far in this chapter. Early Christians and non-Christians understood that Christianity stood or fell based on whether the resurrection happened. From their earliest days in the New Testament, the church of the first century held fast to the belief that the tomb was empty because Jesus was alive. No other explanation fit the facts, in their view.

CONCLUSION

This chapter has barely scratched the surface of evidence for the resurrection. But even in this brief discussion, we have seen how four lines of reasoning converge to prove the truth of the resurrection.

Given the available evidence, the resurrection of Christ is an invitation to a world in which God reigns, Jesus wins, and all that is wrong with this cursed world is made right. It invites us to look beyond the horizon of stubborn unbelief to see a world resplendent with the display of God's handiwork all over it, punctuated by an empty tomb. The resurrection of Jesus invites us to experience resurrection life, a life based on the truth. Nothing could be more rational. Anything less would be irrational.

Chapter Three

FORESHADOWED

THE RESURRECTION
IN THE OLD TESTAMENT

Today's motto seems to be "New is best." Technology is advancing at such a rapid pace that the latest version of a smartphone is outdated within months of its much-anticipated release.

This infatuation with the latest and greatest is not limited to the realm of technological progress. In most areas of scholarship, whether one's work is novel determines its worth in the eyes of the academic establishment. From phones to professors, our culture reserves its highest praise for the latest innovations.

If we apply this motto to the Bible, we find ourselves in trouble. The Bible makes it clear that the New Testament is not superior to the Old Testament. Augustine of Hippo, one of the leaders of the early church, captured the relationship of the two testaments when he wrote, "The new is in the old concealed, and the old is in the new revealed." New is not best in the biblical world. Both testaments are God's Word, and both have much to teach us.

Many Christians would acknowledge the importance of the Old Testament. But those same Christians would admit that reading it is difficult. We enter a foreign world of animal sacrifice and long lists of obscure names we can't pronounce. If we're honest with ourselves, we often ask, "What does the Old Testament have to do with my life in the twenty-first century?"

The simple answer is "Much in every way." For our purposes, however, we face a more urgent question. Isn't the resurrection purely a New Testament reality?

No. The New Testament is unintelligible apart from the Old Testament. So, although reading the Old Testament can be challenging for us, we neglect it to our peril.

Therefore, in this chapter, we will dig into the Old Testament evidence for the resurrection of Christ. Admittedly, it is limited. But that does not mean it is unimportant. As we will see, the few places that refer to the resurrection in the Old Testament are pivotal for our understanding of it. We will begin by taking stock of the general understanding of life after death in the Old Testament. From there, we will unpack the key texts that reveal the resurrection. We will see that the Old Testament foreshadows the resurrection revealed in the New Testament.

LIFE AFTER DEATH?

One of the most persistent questions people have asked in every age is "What happens when we die?" Answers to this age-old puzzle vary wildly. One view is that of certain Eastern religions, which teach that we are reincarnated after death. According to these religions, the state in which we return to this earth is determined by the kind of lives we lived. Another view is that of atheistic materialists, who believe that our physical death is the end of our personal lives. In contrast to both of these options, the faiths that trace their origins to Abraham—Judaism, Christianity, and Islam—all teach some form of personal existence after death.

Since Christianity is a fulfillment of the promises made to Abraham in the Old Testament (Gal. 3:8–9), we will begin with the Old Testament's teaching on life after death. Before we turn to these teachings, we must remember that the Bible is a *progressive unfolding* of God's revelation of Himself. This means that God's disclosure about life after death in the New Testament represents a fullness of revelation that the Old Testament saints did not enjoy.

But we shouldn't conclude that revelation in the Old Testament period is somehow deficient. God is sovereign, so He knows what His people need. And God is good, so He gives His people what they need. Therefore, the progressive nature of God's revelation means that He tells His people what they need to know in every era.

The Old Testament discloses at least three overarching principles on the subject of life after death. First, *death is unnatural.* Death is part of God's curse on creation after the fall (Gen. 3:19). It was an intruder into the garden of Eden, where unbroken fellowship with God was meant to continue forever. This means that Forrest Gump, Tom Hanks' memorable character in the film of the same name, was wrong when he said, "Mama always said, 'Dying is a part of life.'" We were never supposed to go to funerals.

Sin changed everything, for it brought about death. Fellowship with God was replaced by alienation from God. Everlasting life in the garden was exchanged for death in the dust from which man was created. Every mention of death in the Bible from Genesis 3 onward is negative. Death is never seen as something natural, as a part of the cycle of life. Instead, it is always viewed as an enemy to be conquered, not a reality to be accepted (see, e.g., 1 Cor. 15:26).

Second, God's Word teaches that *death does not mean the end of one's personal existence.* Man is body and soul. When he dies, his body returns to the ground, but his soul lives on. We'll list some Old Testament texts in a moment, but I want to use a New Testament text to prove this point.

Jesus tells the story of the rich man and Lazarus in Luke 16:19–31. In this passage, Jesus notes that the rich man went to hades, a term that can sometimes mean the place of the dead but here means hell, as the rich man cries out, "I am in anguish in this flame" (v. 24). By contrast, Lazarus is carried to Abraham's bosom (v. 22).

Remember, Jesus is speaking to a Jewish audience and therefore employs categories familiar to them. His parable summarizes the Old Testament belief that life continued after death and resulted in one of two destinies, either in hades or at Abraham's side—what we would call hell or heaven, respectively.

Third, *there is a distinction between the destinies of the righteous and the unrighteous in the Old Testament.* As one scholar explains, "There are passages, particularly in the Psalms, which express the confident hope for the believing child of God beyond the grave, in distinction from the wicked who go down to Sheol under the wrath of God."[1] This author then lists Scriptures, including Job 19:25–27 and Psalms 1:6; 7:10; 37:18; and 73:24–26. Therefore, the either-or fate of all humankind—heaven or hell—is not merely a New Testament doctrine. It is not an innovation. It is rooted in the Old Testament and developed into its fullness in the New Testament.

Once again, a New Testament passage illustrates this third principle. When Paul is brought before the pagan governor Felix, he tells Felix that his beliefs were accepted by the other Jews present: "I worship the God of our fathers, believing everything laid down by the Law and written in the Prophets, having a hope in God, which these men themselves accept, that there will be a resurrection of both the just and the unjust" (Acts 24:14–15). Like Jesus, Paul believed that our lives continue after death and that we are destined for either heaven or hell.

In light of these three principles, the Old Testament's view of life after death is the same as the New Testament's teaching on the subject. This is what we would expect, given that God is the Author of the entire Bible and He is the same yesterday, today, and forever.

Still, the Old Testament's view of life after death requires the revelation found in the New Testament to gain a complete picture. The Old Testament was *incomplete*, but it was not *incomprehensible* or *inconsistent* with what would be revealed later.

Think about it like this. Have you ever been engrossed in a good story? You can't wait to find out what happens next. You stay awake—you, the lamp, and the book. As you finish the story, all kinds of questions remain, but the main contours of the plot are clear. And they are compelling. You log on to the publisher's website to see if the author has a sequel planned.

Allowing for the imperfections of analogy, the Old Testament is like that. The main parts of the story—including the resurrection—are clear, but the original readers were left waiting for the sequel. Unlike most sequels, however, the New Testament turned out to be as good as the first installment!

RESURRECTION BEFORE JESUS?

Now that we have a general understanding of the Old Testament's doctrine regarding what happens after we die, we'll look at a few texts that foreshadow the resurrection of Christ. Again, the resurrection was revealed in types and shadows in the Old Testament. As a result, these texts do not seem to spell out the resurrection in explicit terms. But this lack of explicit witness to the resurrection is more imagined than real, as we will see.

Moreover, other Old Testament passages prophesy the resurrection in explicit terms. They make it apparent that the promised Messiah would not just conquer Israel's foes. He would do the much more important work of conquering the last enemy, death.

Let's start with Psalm 16:10. David, inspired by the Holy Spirit, writes, "For you will not abandon my soul to Sheol, or let your holy one see corruption." David's words are striking. He articulates a hope of life beyond the grave for himself. He is the Lord's anointed king, and therefore he is the "holy one" referred to in this passage. One thousand years or so before Jesus walked the earth, His ancestor King David hoped in his own resurrection.

Then again, David is not writing simply as Israel's king. He is also writing as a prophet. How do we know this? Because Paul, preaching at the synagogue in Antioch, tells us as much.

Paul explains, "And we bring you the good news that what God promised to the fathers, this he has fulfilled to us their children by raising Jesus" (Acts 13:32–33). Paul supports his argument with an appeal to various psalms, including Psalm 16:10. "And as for the fact that he raised him from the dead, no more to return to corruption, he has spoken in this way, 'I will give you the holy and sure blessings of David.' Therefore he says also in another psalm, 'You will not let your Holy One see corruption'" (Acts 13:34–35).

Paul's use of the Old Testament in this sermon is interesting. Before we can comprehend *how* Paul uses the Old Testament, we need to pause and notice what he believes the Old Testament *is*. In a word, he believes it is the very Word of God. The Lord may have employed human authors and their various idiosyncrasies, but for Paul and the other New Testament authors, what the Bible says, God says. (This understanding wasn't novel to Paul and the other Apostles; Jesus also saw the Old Testament as God's Word, as numerous passages demonstrate.)

Taking Scripture as God's inerrant Word is at odds with so much prevailing scholarship today—even, sadly, in evangelical circles. But the true disciple of Jesus knows that if he wants to follow his Lord, he must hold the same view of inspiration taught by Christ and His Apostles.

Second, Paul connects various psalms to Jesus, though all of them seem to be unrelated to the Messiah's work at first glance. However, they *are* all, in fact, related to Jesus in the sense that the Old Testament's focus and center is Christ. Certainly, some passages (like Ps. 16:10) are more explicitly Christ-centered than others. Yet Jesus Himself makes it clear that the *entirety* of the Old Testament is about Him (Luke 24:27).

Given this, the Apostle tells us that Psalm 16:10 should be understood in light of Christ's resurrection. Paul drives this point home in Acts 13:36–37: "For David, after he had served the purpose of God in his own generation, fell asleep and was laid with his fathers and saw corruption, but he whom God raised up did not see corruption." In other words, David's death proves Paul's point. If David were thinking only of himself, the psalm wouldn't make sense. Therefore, Psalm 16:10 is a prophecy about Jesus and not just David's expression of his hope for life beyond the grave.

A second Old Testament text that hints at the resurrection is Ezekiel 37:1–14. In this passage, God commands the prophet to cry out to a valley of dry bones (v. 4). Ezekiel does as he is told, and the bones take on muscles and flesh before his very eyes, transforming from dry bones into a living army (vv. 7–10). God explains to the astonished prophet that these resurrected warriors are the house of Israel. It is a prophecy of what God will do for His people in the future.

Ezekiel's vision offers us a glimpse of the coming resurrection in two different directions. In one direction, this text declares a *spiritual* rebirth (v. 14) for God's people. But, in the other direction, this spiritual rebirth is accompanied by *physical* resurrection. Flesh and bone were not just convenient metaphors here but rather expressed (again, in an incomplete sense) the hope that God's people would come to life spiritually *and* physically.

Maybe the clearest resurrection text in all the Old Testament is Daniel 12:2, which reads, "And many of those who sleep in the dust of the earth shall awake, some to everlasting life, and some to shame and everlasting contempt." Even on a surface reading, the prophet is clearly talking about a resurrection.

Written hundreds of years after Psalm 16:10, Daniel's vision of a future resurrection is more focused than previous Old

Testament Scriptures on this subject. Interestingly, Daniel seems to be prophesying not about the resurrection of the Messiah in particular but about the resurrection of the dead in general, when Christ returns. But as we explained in the introduction of this book, the two cannot be separated.

The context and genre of Daniel's vision aid us in understanding how this text relates to the resurrection of Jesus. His context is a world of outlandish creatures and prophecies with fulfillments far in the future. Like a lot of the Old Testament, it all seems peculiar to the modern reader.

Here's where understanding the genre of different biblical books plays a key role in comprehending their various meanings. The book of Daniel belongs to the genre called apocalyptic literature. This kind of writing describes what will happen at the end of time using vivid imagery that would have been familiar to the original audience. However strange it may seem to our modern sensibilities, this genre utilizes highly symbolic descriptions to teach God's truth in concrete forms.

When we take the genre into consideration, the general message of Daniel is clear. At the risk of oversimplification, we could summarize that message in this way: God will deliver His people from exile, world history is in His hands, and the Messiah whom God sends will be a human-divine figure who accomplishes a far greater "return from exile" than Israel ever dared to imagine. This divine messianic King will have worldwide dominion, not just kingship over Israel (Dan. 7:14, 22).

For our purposes, Daniel's prophecy of a coming resurrection provides us with a clear Old Testament example of the hope for God's people. Later biblical writers build on this foundation, so

Daniel's words are not an opaque prediction that remains unintelligible for all the ages. Instead, they are a clear indication in Daniel's time that a day of reckoning was coming. This day would be one of great joy or great sorrow, depending on one's destiny. But it would be a day of resurrection, whatever the outcome for those who were raised from the dead.

As a text that describes the general resurrection, Daniel 12:2 provides perhaps the most precise example in all the Old Testament of the hope of resurrection. But how does this text that speaks of the fate of humanity relate to the resurrection of Christ? At its core, any discussion of the resurrection must recognize that *resurrection in the Old Testament was never divorced from a covenantal context.*

This may sound technical, so let's break it down. In both Psalm 16:10 and Daniel 12:2, resurrection occurs in the context of God's keeping His promises to His covenant people. Put another way, the resurrection in the Old Testament was not simply a *general* idea but a *specific* hope that was grounded in God's past revelation of His covenant faithfulness.

Recall that God's covenant is summarized in these words: "I will be their God, and they shall be my people" (Jer. 31:33; Rev. 21:3). What does this promise mean? It means that He bound himself to His people.

Long before these promises to Jeremiah and John the Apostle, God appeared to Abraham in an awe-inspiring scene (Gen. 15:1–21; Heb. 6:13–18). He had Abraham arrange two aisles of slain animals, and He passed through them in the form of a smoking firepot and a flaming torch. The point of this ceremony was to show Abraham that if God were to break His covenantal promises, He would become like the slain animals.

Of course, it is impossible for God to die. But that's the point. In terms of His covenant promise, because it is impossible for God to *die*, it is impossible for God to *lie*. He will keep His promises to His chosen ones without fail. God's covenant is at the very heart of the gospel!

Maybe you've experienced the pain of someone breaking a major promise to you. Your parents weren't good parents. Your spouse walked out on you. That promotion never materialized, even though you were told you were a shoo-in for it. We've all had to come to grips with the fact that people don't keep their word.

Cynicism would be understandable at this point. After all, why trust anyone when promises seem so cheap?

The Bible calls us in a different direction.

Beginning with the Old Testament, we meet a God who keeps His promises. We are introduced to someone we can count on, someone who will never let us down. In a nutshell, *dependability* is at the heart of the covenant. Unlike so many other people or institutions in our lives, we can count on God to do what He says.

With this covenant history of resurrection in view, the Old Testament connection with Christ's resurrection becomes plain. As we have seen, David, the king of Israel who foreshadowed the Messiah, articulates his hope of resurrection in his capacity as the leader of God's covenant people. Daniel, as God's appointed prophet to God's covenant people in exile, broadens David's original prophecy to the whole of humanity.

Once again, God's revelation doesn't come all at once, and it becomes clearer as history progresses. The messianic King's resurrection would be part of a larger story, one that Daniel shows will one day involve the entire human race.

When we gather these various ideas together, a picture emerges. We learned from Psalm 16:10 that the messianic King who comes will be One whom God raises from the dead. Daniel reveals there will be a general resurrection unto judgment or life, in which God's covenant people are rescued by the Son of Man who comes on the clouds (Dan. 7:13–14).

Even from just these two Old Testament passages, we gain an almost word-for-word understanding of the general outline of Jesus' person and work described in the New Testament. For a representative example in the New Testament where both of these ideas are present, look no further than Matthew 25:31–46. There, Jesus, the messianic King foreshadowed in Psalm 16:10, judges the nations in all His resurrection glory in the context of the general resurrection prophesied in Daniel 12:2.

In the end, the Old Testament is remarkable in its prefiguring of what Jesus the Messiah would do, especially when it comes to His resurrection and the resurrection of all humanity in general. Both an *individual resurrection* of the messianic King in Psalm 16:10 and a *general resurrection* of all mankind in Ezekiel 37:1–14 and Daniel 12:2 (cf. Luke 14:14; John 5:29) are taught in its pages. Although these two realities come to us in shadowy form in the Old Testament, they were nevertheless clear enough to ground the old covenant saints' hope. How much more should we who enjoy the complete canon of Scripture rejoice!

RESURRECTION IN THE BOOK
OF EXODUS?

There is one final Old Testament text that figures in to our discussion. Had it not been for Jesus' interpretation of it, though, I think most of us would never have taken it to point to the resurrection of the dead.

Exodus 3:14 is fundamental to understanding the Old Testament as a whole. In an unforgettable scene where a bush burns without being burned up, God reveals Himself as the great I Am, the eternal One who has no beginning and no end. That's what the burning bush symbolized. The Lord discloses His sacred name in the context of Moses' call to lead His people. "God said to Moses, 'I AM WHO I AM.' And he said, 'Say this to the people of Israel: "I AM has sent me to you."'"

Overstating the importance of this text for subsequent biblical revelation would be difficult. Everything that follows is based on what this verse teaches us about God. However, at first blush, this passage seems to have nothing to do with the resurrection. But Jesus demonstrates to us that it has everything to do with the resurrection.

Fast-forward about fifteen hundred years from Moses' world-changing encounter with Yahweh in the wilderness of Midian. Jesus was nearing the end of His earthly ministry. He was being challenged by various Jewish sects about His claims and His teaching. One after another, they tried to catch Him with His own words. They all failed.

Then came the Sadducees. They were, roughly speaking, the theological liberals of Jesus' day. They fancied themselves to have the ultimate argument against what they perceived was Jesus' misunderstanding of Scripture.

They only accepted the first five books of Moses as God's Word, so they turned to a passage from Deuteronomy that lays out the instructions for Israelite remarriage if the husband died. God gave this law to protect the inheritance of widows in Israel, as women at that time would have been among the most vulnerable people in society. Deuteronomy 25:5 reads: "If brothers dwell together, and one of them dies and has no son, the wife of the dead man shall not be married outside the family to a stranger. Her husband's brother shall go in to her and take her as his wife and perform the duty of a husband's brother to her." This was a practice known as levirate marriage.

The Sadducees seized on this law to test Jesus. Here's their argument from Matthew 22:23–28:

> The same day Sadducees came to him, who say that there is no resurrection, and they asked him a question, saying, "Teacher, Moses said, 'If a man dies having no children, his brother must marry the widow and raise up offspring for his brother.' Now there were seven brothers among us. The first married and died, and having no offspring left his wife to his brother. So too the second and third, down to the seventh. After them all, the woman died. In the resurrection, therefore, of the seven, whose wife will she be? For they all had her."

If we put the argument in more formal logical terms, we can see even more clearly what the Sadducees were saying:

1. God's law provides for levirate marriage.
2. Therefore, the seven brothers married the same woman in obedience to God's law.
3. If the resurrection occurs, the seven brothers will be married to the same woman at the same time.

4. God's law prohibits a woman from being married to multiple men at the same time.

5. Therefore, if seven brothers are married to the same woman at the same time, God's law will be violated (from proposition 4).

6. Therefore, if the resurrection occurs, obedience to God's law will result in violation of God's law (from propositions 2, 3, 5).

7. Obedience to God's law cannot result in violation of God's law.

8. Therefore, the resurrection will not occur (from propositions 6, 7).[2]

Stated in this technical format, the Sadducees' argument seems irrefutable.

Their intent was obvious. The masses considered Jesus a great rabbi, and they held the words of Moses in highest regard. To force the issue, the Sadducees tried to create a dilemma by showing everyone in Jerusalem that Jesus was opposed to the law of Moses. If they succeeded, it would have been a crushing blow to Christ's ministry.

Jesus' reply indicates His genius. His answer could not have been more devastating to the Sadducees' reasoning or more enlightening for His followers. We will consider it, step by step.

Before we do, notice something that is easy to miss. *Jesus used logic.* So often, true spirituality and rigorous thinking are set at odds with each other. It is popular to argue that if we are really in tune with our spiritual side, we get there only by short-circuiting our rational faculties. Or we are told that Jesus was opposed to logic and logical reasoning, that He cared only about love, not doctrine.

Nothing could be further from the truth. Not only did Jesus employ very tight logical reasoning in His encounters with the Sadducees, but He did so almost every time He was questioned. The reason (pardon the pun) that Jesus, well, *reasoned* is that reason comes from God. He made us to think logically. In fact, all of us use arguments like the one outlined above on a daily basis. So, being pro-reason does not mean being anti-God.

But we're getting off track. How does Jesus respond to the Sadducees' fallacious argument? Like a good logician, He exposes their mistaken assumptions. Proposition 3 from the syllogism above is the problem. The Sadducees assumed that marriage continued after death. Jesus refutes this notion with a brilliant and surprising argument.

He doesn't sugarcoat His repudiation of their mistaken appeal. "You are wrong, because you know neither the Scriptures nor the power of God," He begins (Matt. 22:29). We need to appreciate how insulting it would have been for the Sadducees to hear these words. They were the ancient equivalent of the Harvard Divinity School faculty. They knew the law of Moses better than anyone alive. So, for them to hear that they did not *actually* know God's Word would have been offensive in the extreme.

But Jesus wasn't engaged in rhetorical name-calling when He said this. He demonstrated that the Sadducees actually didn't understand the Scriptures when He moved from their unfounded specific notion that marriage continues after death to their broader conceptual problem.

Here's where our Lord's argument catches us off guard. He

says that the Sadducees should have known better *because of the tense of the Hebrew verb in Exodus 3:14.* No one saw this coming, least of all the learned Sadducees.

As an aside, we can see in this passage something like what we witnessed in Paul's use of the Old Testament, in that Jesus held to the strongest view of Scripture possible. He believed that the very tenses of the verbs employed by the biblical authors were inspired by the Holy Spirit. We, therefore, should also treat the Scripture with such regard.

Turning our focus back to Jesus' refutation, in telling the Sadducees that marriage ends at death, He used another biblical example. He told them that believers are like the angels, who neither marry nor are given in marriage. So the comprehensive biblical witness was against them.

To be sure, our Lord's reply does not mean that marriage is of no real significance. Elsewhere, Christ teaches us that it is God's good and highest design for those who are called to it (Matt. 19:4–6). Marriage is one of God's gifts to be celebrated, not something to be shunned simply because it is temporary.

But we may be giving the Sadducees too much credit. I don't think they were concerned to understand biblical marriage. They weren't trying to interpret God's law carefully and responsibly. Instead, they wanted to discredit Jesus—nothing more, nothing less.

Even after their erroneous conception of marriage was exposed, the central question remained. How does Exodus 3:14 make it clear that levirate marriage does not violate the law of Moses? Jesus' inference from this text catches us off guard and then sets us on the right path.

His counterargument went like this: Because God is the great

"I Am" of Abraham, Isaac, and Jacob, Jesus argued that He is *still* the God of Abraham, Isaac, and Jacob. God did not tell Moses He *was* the God of these men but said that He *is* their God.

How could this be, since they died *physically* long before Moses wrote Exodus 3:14? Jesus said that if God could still be called their God, then Abraham, Isaac, and Jacob were still alive after death.

If we stop and think about it, Jesus' conclusion from Exodus 3:14 makes perfect sense. One of the central texts of the Old Testament sows the seeds of resurrection in the most unlikely fashion. To put a fine point on His argument, He concludes, "He is not God of the dead, but of the living" (Matt. 22:32). In this encounter with the Sadducees, Jesus shows why He is the epitome of Psalm 119:99: "I have more understanding than all my teachers, for your testimonies are my meditation."

Jesus' reasoning leaves us speechless because He undoes the Sadducees' seemingly airtight logic with simple yet irrefutable reasoning. At any rate, those listening to Him were left without words. "And when the crowd heard it, they were astonished at his teaching" (Matt. 22:33). Whenever I read this passage, it reminds me that I can miss the obvious, even when it is staring me in the face.

There are few movies that illustrate missing the obvious better than the 2006 film *The Illusionist*, starring Edward Norton and Jessica Biel. I won't spoil it for you if you haven't seen it, but there appears to be a tragic ending and a lot of useless details to get the viewer there. But then, the director walks the audience back through various scenes that led them to that point in the film. As this happens, the viewer realizes he missed the obvious all along.

That's precisely what Jesus does here. The Sadducees (and

probably a large majority in the crowd) had read Exodus 3:14 many times. But they didn't tease out its implications. Consequently, Jesus' refutation contains a warning to us as we study the Old Testament. There's always more to God's Word than we can fathom, which increases the danger of missing the obvious.

The primary way to make sure that we don't go down the same blind alley as the Sadducees is to know the Scriptures and the power of God. Stated differently, when we study the Bible, we must humble ourselves before God and confess we are ignorant compared to Him. Only when this is our posture will we truly learn from God and avoid the Sadducees' biblical, not to mention logical, blunders.

CONCLUSION

In this chapter, we began by looking at some basic principles revealed in the Old Testament that shed light on what happens after death. From there, we examined a few key texts from the Old Testament and found that the resurrection is not simply a New Testament reality. It was prophesied hundreds of years before Jesus was even born. In addition, we have seen that Jesus' and the Apostles' use of the Old Testament presents us with the highest view of Scripture possible. Therefore, we can conclude that the resurrection of Christ—and our future resurrection—is not a novelty. It is a story with a long history of hope.

Chapter Four

FULFILLED

THE RESURRECTION
IN THE GOSPELS

All of us have done it. We've said to our spouse or friends or family (usually in an offhand manner), "I'll be there at 5:30." Then we show up at 5:45—or later. Now, for a casual event, most of our acquaintances think nothing of it.

But sometimes our tardiness is evidence of a more serious problem. If we promise our children we'll be home at a certain time and we're always late, then we have become chronic promise breakers. Keeping our word in the seemingly little things (like being on time) demonstrates a concern not only for others' time but also for the truth. In short, we want to be men and women who keep our promises.

In the last chapter, we surveyed the Old Testament evidence for Christ's resurrection. The specific texts pointed to the truth that God keeps His promises that He made in the Old Testament. In this chapter, we'll examine the resurrection accounts in the Gospels and the book of Acts. These are records of God's faithfulness to His pledges in the Old Testament that the Messiah would conquer death and reign forever.

As we'll discover, the New Testament is, in one very important sense, a story about a God who does what He says He is going to do. After sketching the resurrection accounts in the Gospels and Acts, we'll bring the chapter to a close with some concluding observations.

ONE RESURRECTION, FOUR GOSPELS

The four Gospels' accounts of Jesus' resurrection unapologetically claim to be historical. Contrary to popular sentiment, the authors did not believe they were realizing the best of their inner spiritual lives. Still less did they believe they had seen a hallucination when they met the risen Jesus. Instead, each of the four Gospel accounts treats Jesus' return from the grave as something monumental because it actually happened. We must never forget this as we read and reread the Gospels.

We must also keep in mind that the Gospel records, because they were written by eyewitnesses, differ in their reports of some of the details. This should come as no surprise. If three people witness a dramatic event, like a car accident, chances are that each will notice different facts when they recount the crash. These variations do not cast doubt on the event itself but simply highlight that we see things differently.

The same is true in the Gospels' record of Jesus' resurrection. Though God is the ultimate Author of Scripture (2 Tim. 3:16),

His primary authorship does not mean that the human authors were transcriptional robots. The Gospel writers had differing personalities, callings, and experiences. So, they understandably recorded different aspects of the resurrection.

As we study what the Gospels teach us about Jesus' resurrection, we will focus only on the actual accounts of the resurrection of Jesus. Many other parts of Matthew, Mark, Luke, and John refer to it, but unpacking all those texts would demand a book of its own.

Matthew

Matthew's account of the resurrection is found in 28:1–10. After Jesus was buried and guards were assigned to secure the tomb, the unexpected happened:

> Now after the Sabbath, toward the dawn of the first day of the week, Mary Magdalene and the other Mary went to see the tomb. And behold, there was a great earthquake, for an angel of the Lord descended from heaven and came and rolled back the stone and sat on it. His appearance was like lightning, and his clothing white as snow. And for fear of him the guards trembled and became like dead men. But the angel said to the women, "Do not be afraid, for I know that you seek Jesus who was crucified. He is not here, for he has risen, as he said. Come, see the place where he lay. Then go quickly and tell his disciples that he has risen from the dead, and behold, he is going before you to Galilee; there you will see him. See, I have told you." So they departed quickly from the tomb with fear

and great joy, and ran to tell his disciples. And behold, Jesus met them and said, "Greetings!" And they came up and took hold of his feet and worshiped him. Then Jesus said to them, "Do not be afraid; go and tell my brothers to go to Galilee, and there they will see me."

Let's consider a few of the major details from this passage. First, the resurrection quite literally rocked these first witnesses' world. Earthquakes, lightning, and angels—can you imagine a more dazzling scene? No wonder the guards who saw and heard these things "became like dead men" (v. 4)! Remember, these were the warrior elite of the Roman Empire. They probably thought they had seen more than most of us can imagine as they battled to protect Rome's interests. But nothing prepared them for what they saw that first Easter morning.

Second, the resurrection was unexpected. These women did not come to the tomb thinking Jesus wouldn't be there. Twice they were told, "Do not be afraid." This repeated warning indicates that they were shaken by fear.

And who wouldn't be! Their surprise at the resurrection reminds us that the original witnesses were not dupes. They weren't suffering from overheated expectations when they made their way to the tomb that morning. Their shock at Jesus' absence from the tomb only reinforces our claim that we are reading an eyewitness account, not a fabricated legend.

Third, their faith was immediate, and so was their joy (v. 8). Unlike Thomas (whom we'll look at in more detail below), these first resurrection witnesses did not doubt. Instead, they responded in the only appropriate way. They worshiped (v. 9)!

The same two options confront us today. We can either remain skeptical or begin worshiping. Our choice must be one or the other. Indeed, by putting the account of the guards and the women side by side, Matthew forces us to choose which one we will believe.[1]

According to Matthew and the other Gospel writers, the resurrection is of such significance that we must decide immediately what we are going to do with it. Will we follow the women from the empty tomb to trembling, joyful faith? Or will we deceive ourselves that cool, detached suspicion is somehow the only rational posture?

Doubt may be popular today, but when we meet the risen Christ as these women met Him, our knees buckle. Our minds surrender. That which seemed so reasonable—skepticism about miracles—now seems irrational. And the confession that seemed irrational—Jesus is alive!—now seems like the most reasonable, beautiful creed we've ever heard.

One final observation from Matthew's gospel. The fact that women were the first witnesses to Jesus' resurrection only strengthens the argument that we are reading eyewitness testimony. As one scholar observes, "Most of Jesus' Jewish contemporaries held little esteem for the testimony of women."[2] In other words, if you were trying to start a new religion in the ancient Near Eastern world, you wouldn't make women the first witnesses to the crowning miracle of that new religion! Once again, the biblical narrative has the ring of truth to it.

Mark

The gospel of Mark reads more like an action movie script than a modern biography. Written for a predominantly Roman audience, it features snapshots of Jesus' life and ministry. They are woven together by Mark's favorite word, "immediately." Given this fast-paced narrative style, Mark's account of the resurrection is, unsurprisingly, the shortest of the four Gospels'.

Furthermore, Mark 16:9–20—the last verses of his gospel—is one of the most contested passages in the New Testament (the other main disputed text is John 7:53–8:11). Scholars debate whether these verses were part of Mark's original manuscript. I personally think that they were. But even if they weren't, their absence does not affect our understanding of Mark's resurrection narrative in verses 1–8:

> When the Sabbath was past, Mary Magdalene, Mary the mother of James, and Salome bought spices, so that they might go and anoint him. And very early on the first day of the week, when the sun had risen, they went to the tomb. And they were saying to one another, "Who will roll away the stone for us from the entrance of the tomb?" And looking up, they saw that the stone had been rolled back—it was very large. And entering the tomb, they saw a young man sitting on the right side, dressed in a white robe, and they were alarmed. And he said to them, "Do not be alarmed. You seek Jesus of Nazareth, who was crucified. He has risen; he is not here. See the place where they laid him. But go, tell his disciples and Peter that he is going before you to Galilee. There you will see him, just as he told you." And they went out and fled from the tomb, for trembling and astonishment had seized them, and they said nothing to anyone, for they were afraid.

Similarities abound between the accounts in Matthew and Mark. In keeping with Mark's style, the ending is abrupt. But one cardinal difference separates the two records: "and Peter" (v. 7). They are just two words, and they're easy to miss, as they appear to be a minor aside. But these two words make a major theological point.

Why would Mark include these two words from Jesus? Most commentators agree that Mark was recording Peter's eyewitness report of Jesus' life. Imagine how ashamed the great Apostle must have felt while retelling the details of his betrayal just days before (found in 14:66–72)!

Then try to conceive of the overwhelming delight that must have rushed over Peter when the women came and repeated Jesus' words to him. We can picture Peter's big fisherman's frame shaking with sobs. Jesus was alive, and He had forgiven Peter! As we'll see in John's gospel, our Lord would seal Peter's pardon over breakfast.

Mark's narrative of the resurrection reminds us again of the biblical authors' concern for historical accuracy over literary beauty. He walks the reader through the details of Jesus' return from the grave as a reporter would try to summarize a news story. He does not embellish details. He avoids ornate language. Instead, he simply reports the (glorious) events.

Though written in a clipped style, the report Mark passes on to us is not dry or bookish. It offers us unexpected hope in two words. If God can show grace to failures like Peter, then He can show grace to us too. Just as this grace gave hope to Peter, it should give hope to us!

In fact, the gospel of resurrection is summarized in the words "and Peter." Jesus' tender care for sinners comes through in those words. In His resurrection, He had just accomplished the most world-altering feat in the history of the human race. But His concern was for the one who had betrayed Him three times during His night of greatest suffering.

Lest we lose sight of this simple fact as we read these accounts, we must remember that we will never meet another God like Jesus. The gods of other religions are either uninterested in human affairs or too involved with human affairs to be worthy of worship. For example, on the one hand, it would be beneath Allah to become human, die, and rise from the dead. On the other hand, the Greek and Roman gods slept around and got drunk.

In contrast to these two extremes, in Jesus we are introduced to the God who is both above us and with us. In a strange way, Jesus' sinlessness does not repel sinners like us. It invites us and welcomes us. It entreats us to come to Him, the only One who can give us the righteousness we need to stand faultless before the holy Judge we will all face one day.

As if that were not enough, it gets better. Not only did He take our sin upon Himself on the cross, but He also seeks out the Peters of the world. He loves failures when they seem unlovable— even to themselves. They are on His mind, so to speak. What astonishing love! How different is the gospel from anything else the world has to offer!

So, Mark's account is brief but powerful. It tells us about Jesus' resurrection. Furthermore, it offers us grace beyond anything we expected. The miracle of our Lord's victory over death is only magnified by His words "and Peter."

Luke

Scholars generally agree that Luke was one of the great historians of antiquity. At the outset of his gospel, he states that one of his primary goals is an accurate narrative of Jesus' life, death, and resurrection. "It seemed good to me also, having followed all things closely for some time past, to write an orderly account for you, most excellent Theophilus" (Luke 1:3). For the rest of the book, Luke provides the reader with a meticulous description of Jesus' activity while He ministered on this earth.

Luke's account of the resurrection is the most detailed of the four Gospels'. Occupying forty-nine verses in an English translation are some particulars that we do not find anywhere else. While Matthew and Mark speak of only one angel, Luke tells us there were two. This is not a contradiction but is simply a reminder that the Holy Spirit chose what facts each writer would record. The writers didn't each report everything but recorded only the things that God wanted them to hand down to us. Hence, there is no contradiction in the different Gospel accounts of the resurrection.

Given the details in Luke's account, we could miss the resurrection forest for the angelic trees, so to speak, in this text. To help us avoid a myopic reading and thereby obscure the main point, Luke centers our attention on the greatest Bible study ever conducted.

In the church where I have the privilege of being one of the pastors, a group of men has met every week for nearly four decades for a Bible study. They've watched their children—and some of their grandchildren—go from being in diapers to changing diapers. Week by week, they sit and listen to one of the best

Bible expositors in the country go verse by verse through a book of Scripture. These men have learned much, prayed often, and grown significantly in their faith over the years. I praise God for this group!

Examples like these faithful men could be multiplied in churches all over the world. Yet none of these Bible studies can compare to the one on that first resurrection day almost two thousand years ago. A disciple named Cleopas and his friend were walking to a town named Emmaus, which is about seven miles northwest of Jerusalem (Luke 24:13). Suddenly, they were joined by a man who began to travel with them.

They discussed the events of the weekend, and chief among them was the crucifixion of the man who claimed to be God's Messiah. The stranger feigned ignorance as Cleopas summarized what happened. It involved "Jesus of Nazareth, a man who was a prophet mighty in deed and word before God and all the people," he told the stranger (v. 19). In spite of all this, He was crucified.

These two disciples were sorrowful because they had set their hopes on this Jesus (v. 17). As if Jesus' crucifixion weren't bad enough, some of the women had reported that He was alive! This seemed only to add insult to injury. Cleopas and his friend were dejected followers, numb with grief.

What happened next reminds us that Jesus always catches us off guard, just as we saw in His application of Exodus 3:14 in chapter 3. Instead of a comforting "There, there; it'll be all right," Jesus *rebuked* the unbelief of these two men! "O foolish ones, and slow of heart to believe all that the prophets have spoken! Was it not necessary that the Christ should suffer these things and enter into his glory?" (Luke 24:25–26). Jesus diverted their attention from their *grief* to the bigger issue: their *unbelief*. They should have believed the women. More importantly, they should have believed the Scriptures! After all, Jesus explained, the Scriptures taught the necessity of Christ's sufferings and subsequent glory.

Jesus then moved from *admonition* to *instruction*. He guided them through the whole Old Testament (v. 27), teaching them how all of it relates to Him. Seen in this light, Jesus' resurrection illumined their understanding of the person and work of the Messiah as He is progressively revealed in God's Word.

Can you imagine what it would have been like being with Cleopas and his friend on the Emmaus road? To have God the Son instruct you on matters of what to believe about God and what He calls us to do? In a word, we would have been thunderstruck.

We don't need to speculate about what Cleopas and his friend felt, for Luke tells us. Upon entering the village, the three sat down to dinner, and after the blessing, Jesus vanished from their sight! At this point, they knew who was with them. They exclaimed, "Did not our hearts burn within us while he talked to us on the road, while he opened to us the Scriptures?" (v. 32). Blinded eyes gave way to burning hearts.

Such was the power of the resurrection then. But the same Spirit-wrought power is still available today. Our hearts will burn within us as we read the Bible and see Jesus on every page. We can all walk the Emmaus road with Jesus as we study His Word! What a thrill to know that the experience these disciples had is not limited to thousands of years ago in a little town outside Jerusalem. It is offered to weary travelers like us.

One other detail from Luke's account of the resurrection

is worth considering. After their encounter with Jesus on the Emmaus road, Cleopas and his friend shared the details of their earth-shattering Bible study with the other disciples in Jerusalem on the same day (v. 36).

Then, out of the blue, Jesus appeared in their midst, much to their terror. But instead of rebuke, this time He offered assurance. He encouraged His disciples, saying, "See my hands and my feet, that it is I myself. Touch me, and see. For a spirit does not have flesh and bones as you see that I have" (v. 39). Jesus' words here are indispensable for a correct understanding of His resurrection.

Notice, first of all, that He told them that the body He has now is the same one they saw on the cross, except that it is glorified. He made this clear with the emphatic declaration, "It is I myself." As we'll see in the next chapter, there is continuity (as well as discontinuity) between our earthly bodies and our resurrection bodies.

Next, Jesus was adamant that they (and we) understand that His resurrection was a *physical reality*. He was not a ghost. He was not a phantom. He was flesh and blood. He could be touched (see 1 John 1:1–3). He could even eat!

The resurrection makes plain that God calls us to delight in the physical world. Contrary to the ancient Greeks and countless other sects and worldviews, matter is not evil. It was created by God and re-created by Him in the resurrection of Christ. Delicious food, delightful colors, harmonious sounds—all of it was created by God for our delight and His glory (see 1 Tim. 6:17)! By appearing to His disciples in this way, Jesus seals the goodness of the physical world with His nail-pierced hands.

John

No one denies that the fourth gospel differs from the other three, not just in content but in style. It just reads differently than Matthew, Mark, and Luke. Of course, skeptics take this fact and run with it headlong toward unbelief. But, once again, the principle we observed at the start applies here, namely, that we would expect accurate eyewitnesses to offer different details.

Accordingly, several important facts from John's account of the resurrection of Christ stand out immediately. First, John narrates what happens after Mary Magdalene and the other women reported the empty tomb to the other disciples. Peter and "the other disciple" (likely referring to John) returned to the empty tomb with Mary (John 20:3). John reports an important detail that "as yet they did not understand the Scripture, that he must rise from the dead" (v. 9). In their confusion, some of them returned home.

But Mary stayed behind. Again, John is the only one of the four evangelists (as the writers of the Gospels are called) to record Mary's encounter with Jesus. There are many theological implications that follow from this story, but we'll focus on the fact that Jesus appeared to Mary as a gardener (v. 15).

This is not an incidental detail. God once again draws us into the larger story He has been telling in His Word. The book of Genesis reveals that death entered into the world in a garden, when Adam disobeyed God (Gen. 3:1–15). But now, Jesus, the second Adam, has obeyed God perfectly in our place (Rom. 5:12–21). Fittingly, Jesus appeared to Mary as a gardener. As death entered into the world by a gardener in a garden, so to speak, the death of death came into the world in a garden by a gardener.

Mary did not recognize Jesus, even after He spoke to her (John 20:15). Then something almost magical happened. She heard what she thought she would never hear again: the voice of her beloved Savior speaking *her name*. Immediately, the eyes of faith beheld their object! She exclaimed, "Rabboni!" the Aramaic word for "Teacher" (v. 16).

The word Mary used was more than a simple title of honor; its meaning went far deeper. It signified a relational closeness that our translations cannot express adequately. Hence, one scholar writes: "'Rabboni' has a special untranslatable significance. It was the personal response to the personal 'Mary,' to all intents a proper name no less than the other. By speaking it Mary consciously re-entered upon the possession of all that as Rabboni he had meant to her."[3]

Mary wanted this escalated fellowship with her Savior to continue (v. 17). But Jesus said, in effect, "It gets better!" Having ascended to the Father, Jesus ensures through His mediatorial reign that the same closeness Mary experienced in the Easter garden will be offered to all of Jesus' disciples forever!

Two other incidents in John's resurrection account provoke our interest. The first came on the evening of that first Easter. Jesus appeared to the disciples, who were shut up behind locked doors because of their fear (John 20:19). When they realized it was Him, they were glad. But He did not come simply to encourage them. Instead, He commissioned them. Like the episode with Mary, this commissioning takes us back to Eden.

When God created Adam, He breathed life into his nostrils (Gen. 2:7). Just as Jesus undid death in a garden, so He inaugurated the new creation in the same manner as God created mankind. And just as God breathed life into man in the first creation, Jesus breathed life into His disciples at the beginning of the new creation brought about by His resurrection, saying, "Receive the Holy Spirit" (John 20:22).

From that point on, all who believe in Jesus receive the Holy Spirit. That is the symbolic importance of Jesus' action here. We will return to this in chapters 6 and 7, but for now we must simply notice that the Holy Spirit is the Spirit of new creation and resurrection. He is the same Spirit from the first creation (Gen. 1:2). In both cases, the Holy Spirit is the effective agent of creation and re-creation.

In these two vignettes featuring Mary and the disciples, we find ourselves face-to-face with a story that none of us could manufacture from our own resources. The parallels between creation and re-creation, witnessed so plainly in Jesus' encounters with Mary and then His disciples, are inexplicable apart from the view that God sovereignly orchestrated the events of history this way.

What Adam lost in a garden, Jesus restored and made better in a garden. The race that God created good by His inbreathing was reconstituted by the inbreathing of God in the flesh. The good news in both instances is that what Jesus accomplished by His death and resurrection will never be undone. What Adam had was his to lose. Because of His resurrection and ascension, what Jesus gained, He will never lose (John 10:28).

We still must examine one more encounter with Jesus in John's gospel: Jesus' dialogue with Thomas after the commissioning we just discussed. Thomas had been skeptical before the resurrection (11:16), but now his doubt was intractable. He said to the other disciples, "Unless I see in his hands the mark of the nails, and place my finger into the mark of the nails, and place my hand into his side, I will never believe" (20:25). Not only was Thomas a skeptic about the resurrection, but he even laid down conditions to remove his disbelief, conditions that seem impossible to meet.

We can all identify with Thomas, I suspect. As we saw at the outset of our study, we moderns pride ourselves on being scientific people, the kind of folks who don't fall for superstitions like men rising from the dead. But the example of Thomas reminds us that this kind of unbelief is nothing new. It is found right here in one of Jesus' closest companions!

After Thomas set forth his ultimatum of having to see and touch Jesus, we are left with anticipation as we await the climax of this saga. Would Jesus show up? Strike Thomas down for his unbelief? The reader is left in anticipation. What our Lord did next has encouraged doubters for millennia.

Jesus showed up and addressed Thomas personally. The Bible says, "Then he said to Thomas, 'Put your finger here, and see my hands; and put out your hand, and place it in my side. Do not disbelieve, but believe'" (v. 27). The tension we noticed earlier is relieved. Jesus met Thomas where he was, in the midst of what appeared to be stubborn unbelief. Thomas' cool detachment gave way to whole-souled worship. "My Lord and my God!" he exclaimed (v. 28).

Maybe Thomas began that day in a gray cloud of skepticism. Maybe he thought to himself: "My friends are gullible. I'm different. I need proof. No one fools me!" Of course, that's just pure speculation. John doesn't tell us why Thomas didn't believe.

But we do know that Thomas wasn't convinced Jesus was alive, even when his best friends testified to this reality over and over. Then he met the resurrected Jesus. He went from hardened suspicion to exultant worship in an instant. He may have woken up faithless, but he went to sleep that night on the soft pillow of assured belief.

The same transformation can happen to us. We can meet the risen Lord just as Thomas did. In fact, John tells a couple of verses later that the purpose of his gospel is to awaken our faith in Christ: "These are written so that you may believe that Jesus is the Christ, the Son of God, and that by believing you may have life in his name" (v. 31).

Thomas found life in Jesus' name. So can we. That's because the One in whose name we find life is the One who came back to life in order to make eternal life possible.

How can we come to know Jesus like Thomas did? The Lord tells us in verse 29: "Jesus said to him, 'Have you believed because you have seen me? Blessed are those who have not seen and yet have believed.'" Scholars debate whether the first clause should be translated as a question or an expression of astonishment on Jesus' part (just substitute an exclamation point for the question mark and you'll get the idea). Either way, Jesus' words contain a gentle rebuke to Thomas and to us. In effect, Jesus is saying: "Seeing is not believing. Believing is seeing." A mild reproof is followed by a strong encouragement to faith.

If you find yourself in a place of doubt, let Jesus' words comfort you. He is patient with our halting commitment and our divided hearts. But Jesus' ways are often counterintuitive. We may well think to ourselves when reading this account, "If only I could see Jesus like Thomas saw Him, then I would believe!"

But we have to learn the same lesson Thomas learned. Thomas

could see Jesus *physically*, yet he only saw Jesus *truly* when he beheld the Savior by faith. This is why Jesus pronounces a blessing on those who see on the higher plane of faith.

Thousands of people saw Jesus in the flesh but never truly *saw* Him. Here in this passage, Jesus invites us to see Him for who He really is, which goes far beyond sense perception. He turns our eyes into ears so that by the hearing of faith (Rom. 10:17), we finally see the obvious.

CONCLUSION

Through the course of this chapter, we have seen that the four Gospels read like eyewitness accounts. They read like this because that's what they are. They include or exclude details about this massive event as each writer saw fit under God's guidance.

Now we are confronted with maybe the most important question we will ever ask ourselves: Will we believe it? Plenty of evidence points to the truth of the resurrection. But when all is said and done, what matters is whether we will take God at His word. When we do, we see the truth—recorded so simply, beautifully, and accurately in the Gospel stories—that set the world aflame. Jesus is alive.

Chapter Five

FORWARD

THE RESURRECTION IN
THE BOOK OF ACTS

Benjamin Franklin quipped that the only two certainties in life were death and taxes. Given that movies weren't around in his day, Franklin can be forgiven for omitting a third certainty: the sequel will never be as good as the original. Recently, I came across a list of the forty-five worst sequels ever filmed.[1] Movies like *Staying Alive* (the sequel to *Saturday Night Fever*) and *Home Alone 3* (technically not the sequel, which was pretty bad too) made the list of least favorites.

The author who compiled this list of failed sequels noticed that in almost every instance, they had a common trait: they didn't understand why the original film succeeded. So, they ended up trying to mimic something they didn't grasp in the first place. The results were as predictable as death and taxes.

Unlike these botched follow-ups, the book of Acts, which is part two of Luke's gospel (see Acts 1:1), is every bit as good as the first book. Broadly speaking, it tells the story of the postresurrection advance of Christ's kingdom. Acts starts in Jerusalem and closes in Rome. In between is a very detailed historical record of how the resurrection faith of the disciples made swift advances in the ancient world.

With respect to historical accuracy, Acts stands as one of the most trustworthy ancient documents. But, more importantly, it is part of the Word of God. Therefore, it is the Spirit-inspired narrative of how the resurrection of Christ shaped the early church and its mission.

This chapter will focus on two key aspects of how the resurrection functions in Acts. Specifically, we'll look at the *preaching* of the resurrection in Acts. From there, we'll examine a neglected implication of the resurrection: the ascension of Jesus in Acts.

PREACHING THE RESURRECTION IN ACTS

Numerous scholars have remarked that the book of Acts could be retitled "The Book of the Acts of the Holy Spirit." Luke records the work of the Holy Spirit more than any other New Testament writer does. Accordingly, he opens his second act (pardon the bad pun) detailing how Jesus kept His word by sending the Holy Spirit. Jesus *ascended* to heaven, and the Holy Spirit *descended* to earth.

As an initial matter, *when* the Holy Spirit descended is significant. The disciples were gathered together in prayer when the Spirit came upon them as a mighty rushing wind. If nothing else, the fact that He came during a prayer meeting should signal to us the importance of prayer (Acts 2:2).

Not only is the *when* of the Spirit's descent important, but the *how* of His descent is equally significant. At Jesus' baptism, the Spirit took the form of a dove. In Acts, He manifested Himself by wind and tongues of fire. This is a precise fulfillment of John's prophecy that Jesus would baptize "with the Holy Spirit and fire" (Luke 3:16–17).

The *where* of the Spirit's descent matters too. Luke informs us that devout Jews from every nation were in Jerusalem for the Feast of Pentecost. With no warning, these various people groups heard the gospel in their own languages from supposedly backwater, illiterate Galileans (Acts 2:6–7). The miraculous gift of speaking in known languages contains a subtle but important message for us.

To comprehend its meaning, we need to go back to Genesis 11. There, we read about the Tower of Babel and how God frustrated the plans of sinful man to work their way to heaven by confusing their language.

The effects of God's punishment at Babel live on today. On a recent visit to Eastern Europe, I had the honor of enjoying a meal in the home of a man who spoke at least five languages fluently. His English was flawless, as was his French (though I was an exchange student in France at one point, my French was rusty, to put it diplomatically).

Seeing his library—which included books in Polish, Russian, Arabic, Greek, and English—reminded me that the curse of Babel is still very real. Languages are one of the most significant markers of cultural distinction. Their variety and difficulty to learn are also a daily reminder that God frustrated mankind's design to build a monument to its pride.

This is why the disciples' speaking in known tongues here in Acts 2 is so striking. It reveals to us that God gathers the nations together, not through their work (as they attempted at Babel) but through Christ's work on the cross.

Therefore, with the Spirit's descent, the nations began to hear the language of grace, as it were. Pentecost preaches the gospel to us, in its when, how, and where. It proclaims that we cannot build our way back to God, as the architects of Babel supposed. Salvation comes only by the Spirit's descending to us, not by our attempting to build our way back to God. Pentecost was the initial moment that signified that the Spirit would gather together God's people scattered across the world.

Immediately after this miraculous event, the Holy Spirit deployed the newfound harmony of language for the noblest purpose: preaching the Word of God. The first recorded Christian sermon comes from the lips of Peter (vv. 14–39). His words teach us that the Spirit's primary focus, regardless of the human language He uses, is the "word of the cross" (1 Cor. 1:18) preached boldly in the power He supplies.

When Peter lifted his voice to proclaim the resurrected and ascended Messiah, it was clear that the change in him was nothing short of breathtaking. Gone was the shrinking fisherman, intimidated by a teenager and afraid to stand with Jesus. In his place, the fiery, eloquent Apostle emerged.

As he rivets our attention on Jesus in his sermon, Peter makes clear that Jesus is not a surprise ending to an otherwise Christless story. According to Peter, *all* of the Old Testament is about Jesus.

Peter's use of the Old Testament here reminds us that the original penmen of Scripture were aware that they were looking beyond their times when they wrote their prophecies (Acts 2:16; 1 Peter 1:10–12).

The centerpiece of Peter's sermon is the resurrection of Jesus: "This Jesus God raised up, and of that we are all witnesses" (Acts 2:32). For Peter and the other Apostles, Christianity cannot exist without a resurrected Christ. This sermon demonstrates that the physical fact of the resurrection was a nonnegotiable doctrine from the earliest days of the Christian message.

As we saw in the introduction to this book, the *physical fact* of the resurrection is inseparable from the *theological meaning* of it. Peter's sermon reinforces this conviction. He moves from declaring the resurrection to unfolding its God-given meaning for his hearers. He says that Jesus' resurrection means that Jesus is Lord of all and the promised Messiah (v. 36).

His audience understood the life-changing implications of this statement. Everything depended on how they responded to this message. Therefore, they cry out to Peter and the other Apostles, "Brothers, what shall we do?" (v. 37). Peter's answer is as powerful as it is simple: "Repent" (v. 38).

A similar experience awaits us. When we realize that Jesus is alive, we realize that we are dead in our trespasses and sins (Eph. 2:1). As was the case for the audience in Jerusalem that day, the only hope we have is to turn to Christ in faith and repentance.

Consequently, at the heart of the gospel is another miracle, the miracle of the new birth. This is when a sinner is brought to life by the Holy Spirit (John 3:1–5). Because Jesus is alive, our sins can be forgiven through Spirit-wrought faith that results in

God-given repentance (Eph. 2:8–10). Faith and repentance are, to use the language of the older theologians, two sides of the same coin. They are distinct but inseparable. According to Peter, the only valid response to the resurrection proclamation is to turn from sin in faith in the risen and ascended Messiah.

The Apostolic preaching recorded in the book of Acts that followed Peter's inaugural sermon takes this shape. In Acts 4, we read the account of Peter and John's trial before the Jewish ruling council. Their crime? Peter had healed someone (see 3:7)! Standing trial for their lives, the two Apostles did not waver. They preached the resurrection to the council (4:10), in the power of the Holy Spirit. When told to stop their work, they responded with words that should inspire every Christian. "We cannot but speak of what we have seen and heard" (v. 20).

When we know the resurrection is true, we will have the same confidence exhibited by Peter and John. The truth of the resurrection—and all that it entails—will loosen our tongues and open our mouths in praise and proclamation!

For those united to the resurrected Messiah by faith alone, silence is never an option. There, truth of the resurrection is irresistible! Without fail, our lips follow the lead of our hearts, for good or for ill (Mark 7:21). If we have been changed in our innermost being by the resurrection, then we have no other option than to tell others the good news.

Acts 5 finds the Apostles seized by the authorities yet again. Miraculously, an angel sets them free from prison (vv. 19–20). Peter and the others return to their work of evangelism in the temple (v. 21). When the power brokers demand to know why the Apostles so flagrantly ignored the command not to teach, the

Apostles reply with another bold statement: "We must obey God rather than men" (v. 29).

Notice again the *irresistibility* of the resurrection for the early preachers. Lives, property, status—none of it mattered to them. Since God raised Jesus from the dead, the only response was proclamation. Threats were useless. The heavy bars of a Roman prison could not contain them or their message. Jesus' triumph over the grave made them fearless. It can do the same for us today.

One of my heroes in the faith illustrates how being certain of biblical truths like the resurrection changes our lives. Billy Graham is widely regarded as the greatest evangelist in our lifetime. Early in his fast-growing ministry, his colleague Charles Templeton began to question the authority of Scripture. Templeton shared his doubts with Graham, which set off a series of events that resulted in two vastly different lives.

Templeton left Graham's ministry and did probably the worst thing someone with doubts can do. He went to a liberal theological seminary. His unbelief was only reinforced, and he eventually left not only the ministry but Christianity altogether. Templeton's example stands as an urgent warning for all of us to steward our doubts well, if I can put it like that, lest we end up in total unbelief.

Unlike Templeton, Graham did probably the best thing someone with doubts can do. He took them to the Lord. He wrestled through his questions and came to believe with firm conviction that the Bible is the Word of God.

Shortly after he came to this conclusion, the event that began Graham's worldwide ministry—the 1949 Los Angeles Crusade—took place. We know how the story ends. Strengthened by his belief in the Bible as the Word of God, Graham went on to become arguably the greatest evangelist of the twentieth century.

At the heart of Graham's message was the conviction that the Bible is God's Word. What it says is true, without question. Graham was simply following in the footsteps of Peter. Once convinced that the Bible and the doctrines it teaches—like the resurrection—are true, we will find ourselves irresistibly drawn to proclaiming these amazing truths!

But going back almost two thousand years now and returning to the book of Acts, we meet the Apostle Paul. Within a few chapters after these fascinating events in Acts 5, Luke introduces us to Saul of Tarsus, a man who persecuted the infant Christian church ruthlessly.

Then he met the resurrected Jesus (9:1–19).

From that point on, he became the greatest missionary of all time. He wrote almost half of the New Testament. We would not be going too far if we said that history would not be the same without Paul.

The resurrection of Christ was fundamental to Paul's preaching (13:37; 17:3; 22:8; 24:15; 26:8, 23). We'll examine his theology of resurrection in detail in the next chapter, but for the moment, let's concentrate on how Paul preached the resurrection in Acts. Looking at chapter 17, we find Paul proclaiming the resurrection to a largely unbelieving, non-Jewish audience.

When he was brought before the Areopagus, which was made up of the leading intellectuals of the day, Paul offered them a very Jewish worldview. He began with God as Creator (17:24ff.), a notion that would have been foreign to a predominantly Greek assembly. He then turned their attention to the coming judgment on sin, another completely alien idea (vv. 30–31).

And then Paul made things even more interesting. He told these lettered men of distinction that they could know for certain that a day of judgment is coming *because of the resurrection.* "He has fixed a day on which he will judge the world in righteousness by a man whom he has appointed; and of this he has given assurance to all by raising him from the dead" (v. 31). We could call this the "bad news of the resurrection."

On the one hand, the resurrection is extraordinarily good news for those who believe. On the other hand, it is unspeakably bad news for those who choose not to believe (which many on the fateful day in Athens elected to do; see v. 32). As a result, the resurrection functions as a warning in Paul's preaching here.

When we read Acts 17, it all seems so contemporary. By this, I mean that our society mirrors the one Paul encountered at the Areopagus almost two thousand years ago. Today's Western world sees myriad belief systems, just like Athens in Paul's day. The idea that there is one God in three persons, who made everything and will judge everyone, seems outlandish to many people today, just as it did when Paul addressed the Greek intellectuals two millennia ago.

Maybe the place where we see the most similarity between Paul's time and ours is the shared disdain for the resurrection of Christ. Here's how the original hearers responded: "Now when they heard of the resurrection of the dead, some mocked. But others said, 'We will hear you again about this.' So Paul went out from their midst. But some men joined him and believed, among whom also were Dionysius the Areopagite and a woman named

Damaris and others with them" (vv. 32–34). Luke records three different reactions to the resurrection.

First, we encounter *blatant unbelief.* "Some mocked," Luke tells us. Today, this reaction takes the form of materialistic atheism or militant paganism. Thought leaders scorn Christianity just as they did in Paul's time. They'll take the late physicist Stephen Hawking seriously when he pontificates about hostile aliens. But if you tell them that God's Word is without error, or that Christ's shed blood is the only way to be right with God, or that Jesus walked out of the tomb on the third day, you'll be dismissed as a contemptible fool.

Truly, "there is nothing new under the sun" (Eccl. 1:9). Swelled with false pride because of technological superiority, present-day unbelief imagines itself to be intellectually superior to the mind-set of ancient people. But this episode in Acts 17 reveals that our age is no more advanced intellectually than that of the ancient Greeks to whom Paul preached. Sure, we have cell phones, indoor plumbing, and antibiotics, but we still face hostile unbelief that dismisses the resurrection without even considering it as a live possibility.

Second, there is *apathetic agnosticism.* "We will hear you later." This is the person today who hears the stupendous news of the gospel and responds with a half-hearted "meh." Unfortunately, this may be the most common response to the resurrection, both in Paul's day and in ours. Many people simply don't care about spiritual things. They're not overtly hostile to Christianity. They're not opposed to anything, in fact. They don't commit to people, jobs, or "organized religion." Of course, they'll listen politely. They consider themselves spiritual, in some sense. But they are "always learning and never able to arrive at a knowledge of the truth" (2 Tim. 3:7).

Agnosticism of this variety is mistaken. These people are not simply uncommitted to Christianity; they are opposed to it. After all, as we saw in chapter 1, we're all committed to something. To refuse to commit to Jesus is to decide against Him (Matt. 12:30). According to the Lord, no one is on the fence. Delayed belief like the kind Paul encountered and like what we witness today is just unbelief with window dressing.

The third response is *joyful commitment*. Luke records that "some . . . believed," including one of the members of the Areopagus (Acts 17:34). To many onlookers in this ancient ivory tower, the gospel's victory appeared unremarkable. But if one thing is clear in the book of Acts, it is God's sovereignty over all human history (2:23 summarizes this fact in stunning terms). Those who believed were exactly those whom God "appointed to eternal life" (13:48).

Similar confidence in God's sovereignty should mark our proclamation of the gospel to our culture. Our "success" may not look significant in the world's eyes. But we are not called to win the world's approval. Our job is *proclamation*; the *reception* of the good news is in God's hands. Still, to be faithful to the gospel in an unsympathetic culture, we must keep the resurrection of Jesus central in our preaching and teaching, just as Paul and the other Apostles did.

A NEGLECTED PIECE OF THE PUZZLE

Having surveyed briefly the preaching of the book of Acts, we need to return to a topic mentioned in the introduction to this chapter. One of the most important—and overlooked—facts of the resurrection is the ascension of Christ. We could go so far as to say that Christ's resurrection was *unto* ascension. His ascension and being seated at the Father's right hand (known as His "session") are part of what theologians call the priestly work of Jesus (the other two aspects of His work are the kingly and prophetic offices).

Some context might help. The Scriptures make it clear that Jesus is our Great High Priest who fulfills everything that the priesthood in the Old Testament anticipated (see Heb. 2:17; 3:1; 5:1–10; 6:20). Unlike the priesthood of human high priests, though, Jesus' priesthood is *eternal* and *effectual*. He ever lives to intercede for His people at the Father's right hand (Heb. 7:25)! Therefore, the ascension of Christ is very, very good news for sinners like us.

In addition, the ascension of Christ is itself *the fulfillment of a larger promise*. Throughout Luke's gospel and into the opening chapter of Acts, we read of the "promise of the Father" (Acts 1:4). What is this enigmatic promise?

Luke tells us that the *promise* is actually a *person*, the Holy Spirit. In Luke 24:49, Jesus hints at this reality when He says: "And behold, I am sending the promise of my Father upon you. But stay in the city until you are clothed with power from on high." After the outpouring of the Holy Spirit at Pentecost, during his sermon reviewed earlier in the chapter, Peter could say of Jesus, "Being therefore exalted at the right hand of God, and having received from the Father the promise of the Holy Spirit, he has poured out this that you yourselves are seeing and hearing" (Acts 2:33). Moreover, Paul strengthens this identification between the promise of God and the Holy Spirit in his letter to the Galatians when he informs us that we "receive the promised Spirit through faith" (Gal. 3:14).

The promise of the Spirit is larger than the New Testament, however. It is part of the gospel story going back to Abraham. The full text of Galatians 3:14 reads, "So that in Christ Jesus the blessing of Abraham might come to the Gentiles, so that we might receive the promised Spirit through faith." God's Word equates the blessing of Abraham with the promised Spirit.[2] As a result, when Jesus ascended to the Father's right hand and the Spirit was poured out at Pentecost, it was all happening to fulfill God's promises to Abraham.

A further implication of Jesus' ascension and the Holy Spirit's descent is that the church is *empowered for mission*. We'll discuss this fact in more detail in chapter 7. For now, we will simply draw some connections between these two realities of ascent and descent.

A new era of the Spirit began, so to speak, at Jesus' baptism. As He passed through the baptismal waters, He was undergoing a type of judgment in our place, foreshadowed by the biblical flood (Gen. 7:17–24) and then the Red Sea crossing (Ex. 14:21–29).

Therefore, our Lord's baptism teaches us that Jesus reenacts these water judgments. His baptism was a kind of judgment by water. It signifies that He was judged in our place, foreshadowing the ultimate covenant judgment He would undergo at the cross. Hence, He refers to the cross as a baptism (Mark 10:38).

When He came up from the water, the Holy Spirit descended upon Him in the form of a dove. This was in fulfillment of Isaiah 61:1: "The Spirit of the Lord God is upon me, because the Lord has anointed me to bring good news to the poor; he has sent me to bind up the brokenhearted, to proclaim liberty to the captives, and the opening of the prison to those who are bound."

Jesus drew attention to this fact in His inaugural sermon (Luke 4:16–18). Isaiah was prophesying about a time when God's Suffering Servant would be filled with the Spirit in a unique way. He would bring about the Jubilee that had never materialized in Israel. But this Jubilee year, ushered in by this Spirit-filled Servant, was not a temporal release of debt or slavery. It was an eternal state ushered in by the work of the Messiah.

From Jesus' baptism, to His ministry of healing and teaching, to the cross, to the resurrection (Rom. 1:4), He was the man of the Spirit par excellence. In all His thinking, doing, and living, He was the embodied fulfillment of Paul's admonition to "walk by the Spirit" (Gal. 5:16). What does the fact that Jesus was the Spirit-filled man above any other have to do with the ascension?

Once Jesus was raised from the dead in the power of the Spirit, a categorical shift in the relationship between the Holy Spirit and God's people took place. In the Old Testament, the Spirit's activity was more limited, less defined.

But now, because Jesus has been raised from the dead, a new epoch of the Spirit has begun. The enjoyment of this new time of the Spirit's activity awaited the ascension of Christ. Hence, as we noted at the outset of this chapter, when our Lord *ascended* to heaven as the disciples watched (Acts 1:9–10), it followed almost immediately that the Spirit *descended* at Pentecost (2:4).

The ascension of Christ and the outpouring of the Holy Spirit help us understand Peter's exegesis of an ancient prophecy in his sermon at Pentecost. Peter exclaims, "But this [the outpouring of the Holy Spirit] is what was uttered through the prophet Joel: 'And in the last days it shall be, God declares, that I will pour out my Spirit on all flesh'" (2:16–17). The question foremost in most readers' minds is this: What are the last days, and when are they coming? According to Peter, the last days began at Pentecost! That may catch some readers off guard, so we need to take a brief detour and delve into the New Testament's understanding of history.

When I was in seminary, I worked as a youth pastor. As I was learning how to handle the Word of God (and being fairly young myself), I sought the counsel of a pastor when I was planning my first teaching series for our large-group gatherings. He looked at me and said, "There are two guaranteed topics to get students' attention: sex and the end times." Because this was my first extended series as the church's youth pastor, I decided to go with the end times.

If I thought my decision would avoid controversy, I was mistaken. Few topics are as hotly contested as the end times, so much so that the subject has become a cottage industry in modern evangelicalism, with views ranging on the scale from intriguing to downright fantastical. From the mega-selling *Left Behind* book series (then movies) to anxious predictions of TV "prophets," end-times fascination shows no sign of letting up. Not that this fixation on the last days is limited to current evangelicalism. It has always been there throughout church history.

Despite the church's (and indeed, people's) fascination with the end times, many believers are too intimidated to study anything related to the last days. They feel ill-equipped. Or they have been bulldozed by prophecy experts who assure them that a detailed knowledge of geopolitical affairs is necessary to truly know when Jesus is coming back. As I would discover in the course of my preparation, however, the New Testament teaching on the last days and end times is relatively straightforward, believe it or not.

In essence, Jesus and the Apostles divide history into two ages: "this age" (Matt. 12:32; Mark 10:30; 1 Cor. 1:20; Gal 1:4) and the "age to come" (Matt. 12:32; Mark 10:30; Luke 18:30). The two ages are divided by the return of Christ.

Simple enough. But we must recognize one wrinkle. The age to come breaks into this age in the complex of events made up of the resurrection of Christ, His ascension, and the outpouring of the Holy Spirit. The inbreaking of the age to come is why Peter could claim that his audience two thousand years ago was witnessing the inauguration of the last days prophesied by Joel.

Therefore, to be more precise, a believer lives in this present age but enjoys a *partial fulfillment* of the coming age by the power of the Holy Spirit until the day when Jesus returns and the age to come explodes in all its glorious fullness. In biblical terms, the age to come that breaks into this age is the same thing as "these last days" (Heb. 1:2).

At least two conclusions follow from this quick survey of the last days in Scripture. First, the last days began almost two thousand years ago with Christ's advent, death, resurrection, and ascension combined with the outpouring of the Holy Spirit. Therefore, we have been living in the last days for millennia.

By highlighting this important biblical truth, I am not denying that a time will come when persecutions will arise, widespread apostasy will be the norm, and awful tribulation will mark the life of the church (see Matt. 24:3–14; Rev. 6:1–17) just before the return of Christ. Theologians have long debated the timing and scale of these events, but those details do not need to detain us here. Whenever these events occur, they will indicate that the end is near.

Second, the age to come is the age of the Spirit. Christians enjoy the fruits of the age to come in this age, in union with Christ by the power of the Holy Spirit, as they await the fullness of their redemption in the resurrection of their bodies. This is why the ascension of Christ and subsequent outpouring of the Holy Spirit are so important for our daily lives.

When we struggle against sin or keep persevering in the faith, the Spirit's work in us makes these things possible. In turn, the Spirit's work follows inexorably from Jesus' ascension. Far from being a secondary concern, therefore, the ascension is a vital aspect of our salvation.

Altogether, the resurrection of Christ, His ascension, and the outpouring of the Spirit begin a new period in covenant history. We live in the same era today, with the same resources that were available to the early church.

Our summary of the Spirit's work in our lives in this age has been necessarily brief. But one final implication of Christ's ascension deserves some discussion.

We have seen that the author of Hebrews in particular goes to great lengths to help us understand that Jesus is a High Priest of a different order than the high priests of the Old Testament. While the earthly high priests were descended from Aaron, Jesus' priesthood came from Melchizedek (Heb. 5:5–6), the shadowy Old Testament figure who greeted Abraham in Genesis 14:18–20.

The author of Hebrews goes on to explain the significance of this ancient priest. "He is without father or mother or genealogy, having neither beginning of days nor end of life, but resembling the Son of God he continues a priest forever" (Heb. 7:3). Like other Old Testament figures, Melchizedek prefigured Christ. More astonishingly, the author of Hebrews argues that the Old Testament indicates that a high priest was coming who would not be from Aaron's line. Millennia before Jesus walked the earth, even before Aaron became a high priest over God's people, Melchizedek anticipated Christ's high priestly work.

Like the aspects of the Old Testament world that we studied in chapter 3, the world of high priests and ancient patriarchs like Abraham seems about as far removed from our world today as one could imagine. A moment's reflection, however, will show us that because we live in the last days along with the original readers of the New Testament, Jesus' priesthood is extraordinarily practical.

Here's how Hebrews explains this importance to us: "For we do not have a high priest who is unable to sympathize with our weaknesses, but one who in every respect has been tempted as we are, yet without sin" (4:15; see also 7:26). Because He was sinless, He was not like a human high priest. He did not have to offer a sacrifice for His sins because He was sinless. Instead, He could offer Himself—not bulls or goats—to atone for our sins (7:27). Therefore, "he always lives to make intercession" for us (7:25).

Consequently, the priestly session of Christ at God's right hand should be comforting to us. Have you struggled against a particular sin for years, only to be mastered by it yet again? Jesus was tempted and succeeded where we fail. So, He not only sympathizes with us but also *does something* about our sin. He atoned for it. Therefore, it no longer has power over us (Rom. 6:14). He delights to help weary sinners like us as He carries out His priestly work on our behalf! That's why He invites us who are heavy-laden to come to Him (Matt. 11:28).

Do you wonder if your faith is enough to save you? Because Jesus offered Himself as a perfect sacrifice for our sins as our High Priest, we could not possibly add anything to His work. So, it is not the strength of our faith that saves us but rather the work of the One in whom we place our faith. The author of Hebrews concludes, "Consequently, he is able to save to the uttermost those who draw near to God through him" (Heb. 7:25).

Finally, do you feel like your prayers stop at the ceiling? I know I feel like that sometimes. What a wonderful encouragement to know that Jesus always hears us! This truth should thrill us: Jesus, as our Great High Priest, *prays for us*. As a result, we *know* that our prayers are never in vain. Jesus takes even the feeblest cry to Him and offers it to His Father.

How wonderful are Christ's ascension and priestly session! In God's economy, both are the natural result of the resurrection. Jesus has been raised, the Spirit has been sent, and Jesus lives forever to guide His people through the wilderness of this life as their High Priest. Put simply, one of the best things about being a Christian is that God provides all we need, from start to finish!

CONCLUSION

In this chapter, we have seen that the resurrection of Christ is foundational to the message of the early church. The book of Acts supplies us with multiple examples of this fact. Moreover, we have examined the overlooked doctrine of the ascension to better understand Jesus' priestly work for us. As a gateway to the rest of the New Testament, Acts lays a foundation for understanding all that follows by explaining to us the resurrection of Christ, His ascension, and the outpouring of the Spirit.

Chapter Six

FORETASTE

THE RESURRECTION IN THE NEW TESTAMENT

Few things compare to witnessing the Masters Tournament in person. I had the opportunity to make my first trip a couple of years ago, winding my way through the sunrise on I-20 with a friend who was a Masters veteran. He knew exactly where to go so that we got the full experience.

We entered the course right near the sixteenth hole, and without even realizing it, I stopped walking and took in the moment. It was first thing Friday morning, the sun sprinkled through the storybook pines of Augusta National, and it was about 65 degrees. The iconic yellow flags snapped in the crisp breeze. The smell of pimento cheese and pine straw never left your nostrils. I even thought I heard Jim Nantz say, "Hello, friends," as we unshouldered our green chairs to take our seats at number sixteen ("Redbud").

Though I had watched the Masters for years on TV, nothing prepared me for what I saw in person that spring day in Augusta.

At the risk of overstatement, in that moment I felt like I caught a glimpse of the glory that awaits believers. Augusta National represents an attempt at perfection. From the pines to the greens, everything is (or, at least, *appears* to be) as it should be. In that moment, I was tempted to think, "It can't get any better!"

But the Bible says it does. Even with its seeming flawlessness, Augusta National is still a dim and imperfect pointer toward the consummation of God's handiwork at the end of all things. The Scriptures remind us time and again that in the new heaven and new earth, everything will finally be made whole. Our speculations about perfection will cease, and we will simply bask in it.

In this chapter, we will consider the glory coming to Christians as we finish our overview of the biblical teaching about the resurrection. Our focus will be on two of Paul's letters. We will learn that the resurrection of Christ is a foretaste in the present of the glory to come. It is heaven breaking into earth.

THE RESURRECTION CHAPTER: 1 CORINTHIANS 15

The centerpiece of biblical teaching on the resurrection of Christ and the future resurrection of believers is 1 Corinthians 15:1–58. Countless pages have been written on these verses, but here we will focus on what essentially are the three main teaching sections.

Revelation and Corroboration: 1 Corinthians 15:1–8

Paul begins this chapter by telling us that what follows is the heart and soul of the biblical gospel.

Now I would remind you, brothers, of the gospel I preached to you, which you received, in which you stand, and by which you are being saved, if you hold fast to the word I preached to you—unless you believed in vain. For I delivered to you as of first importance what I also received: that Christ died for our sins in accordance with the Scriptures, that he was buried, that he was raised on the third day in accordance with the Scriptures, and that he appeared to Cephas, then to the twelve. Then he appeared to more than five hundred brothers at one time, most of whom are still alive, though some have fallen asleep. Then he appeared to James, then to all the apostles. Last of all, as to one untimely born, he appeared also to me. (vv. 1–8)

These verses set the stage for everything else that he writes in this chapter. They form the nucleus of Paul's theology of the resurrection, and therefore we need to work through them carefully.

Paul assures us that what he writes is critical to the gospel (v. 1). Christians may differ over some issues, but the resurrection of Christ is not one of them, Paul informs us. In other words, the truth of the gospel depends on whether the resurrection actually happened. Consequently, much is at stake in Paul's words.

The Apostle then reminds us that the gospel he teaches and preaches was delivered to him. He "received it." He did not make it up (cf. Gal 1:11–15). It was not his interpretation of reality. It was and is the direct revelation of God.

These might seem like useless details, but they are the difference between Christianity and everything else. When we open the pages of the world's religions, we read story after story of mankind's trying to work its way back to God. The different faiths of mankind are simply the best inclinations of our common humanity directed toward the spiritual elements of the universe.

Although many people may sincerely hold to such faiths, that does not make their sacred writings true. Apart from God's revelation in the gospel, our spiritual musings do not represent noble strivings after the truth. They indicate a darkened mind that prefers *speculation* to *revelation* (Rom. 1:18–25; Eph. 4:17–19).

Accordingly, we must not downplay or neglect Paul's words here. He makes a breathtaking claim about the gospel, a claim that fundamentally changes the way we relate to God. Paul teaches that the gospel reverses our sinful religious impulse. According to him and the rest of the Bible, we don't work our way back to God; He comes down to us. This is the cornerstone of the good news.

And at the center of this gospel is the resurrection of Christ. It is "of first importance" (1 Cor. 15:3). We could translate this phrase "first and foremost."[1] The resurrection matters that much. Christianity is false if the resurrection is not true, as Paul will go on to argue (vv. 12–17). In a word, Paul's gospel—the biblical gospel—is the gospel of resurrection.

We might be tempted to question how much emphasis Paul places on the resurrection. Isn't he going too far? Putting all his eggs in one basket, so to speak?

The short answer is no, because the gospel is God's revelation. Paul did not determine the emphasis. God did. Paul is simply a messenger.

Surprisingly (and sadly), some churches deny the bodily resurrection of Christ. Viewed from Paul's vantage point here in

1 Corinthians 15, disavowing the resurrection is disavowing the gospel. Again, the stakes could not be higher when it comes to our view of the empty tomb.

This might be a good time to pause and ask ourselves, "Do I believe the same gospel as the Apostle Paul?" It is very easy to deceive ourselves here. We might point to our involvement at church or our regular habit of prayer. Both of those are good, even requisite, spiritual disciplines.

But neither will save us. Nor will any additional spiritual activities. We must believe the biblical gospel to be saved. Simply put, that means we must believe in the bodily resurrection of Jesus.

Not only is the resurrection at the center of the gospel, but it is in "accordance with the Scriptures" (vv. 3–4). Paul mentions this fact twice to drive his point home. As we learned in chapter 3, Jesus' victory over death was foretold by the Old Testament. Paul reiterates that claim here.

By stating it in these terms, Paul brings us face-to-face with the issue of authority. In previous chapters, we saw how the Bible asserts for itself ultimate authority in our lives. When it comes to the resurrection, our allegiance must not be to the pronouncements of scientists or even biblical scholars. We must submit to God's Word above all. His Word is our overarching authority.

Beware of the claim that the Bible's authority amounts to a circular argument at best or pious fiction at worst. As the great theologian Bob Dylan sang, "You're gonna have to serve somebody." All of us have some ultimate authority over our lives. Every worldview has a stopping point, so to speak. Thus, all of us are in the same boat when it comes to our ultimate allegiance.

For example, if someone claims that reason is his prime authority, the question becomes, "How do you know that?" If reason is his king, consistency demands that he answer, "I know this because I reasoned to this conclusion." Of course, this reply isn't really a reason, but it simply begs the question.[2]

Viewed in this light, the question of authority may seem hopeless. But that's where the Bible differs, in a profound way, from other claims to authority. As we have observed over the course of this book, the biblical worldview alone can make sense of reality. In other words, only the Bible can bear the weight of the demands that an ultimate authority makes. Although all worldviews may be in the same boat when it comes to authority claims, only the biblical boat stays afloat.

Therefore, according to Paul, we should believe the resurrection because it is revealed in Scripture. The Bible is the highest authority, not reason or evidence (indispensable as both are). The Apostle's claim is arresting in its simplicity. The resurrection is true because God disclosed it in His Word.

From here, Paul moves from *revelation* to *corroboration*. What evidence confirmed the scriptural doctrine of the resurrection? Four times Paul tells us that Jesus "appeared" after He was raised from the dead. Though Scripture was Paul's highest authority, this commitment did not force him to ignore the evidence for the resurrection. In fact, he *appeals* to this evidence.

The primary support for the reality of Jesus' resurrection was eyewitness testimony. Peter was a witness ("Cephas" is Peter's name in Aramaic). So were James and Paul. So were about *five hundred* other people. In other words, the resurrection was a well-known fact.

When he was brought before a pagan ruler, Paul said as much.

Arguing for the resurrection at an audience with King Agrippa, Paul exclaimed: "For the king knows about these things, and to him I speak boldly. For I am persuaded that none of these things has escaped his notice, for this has not been done in a corner" (Acts 26:26). The resurrection of Jesus was well attested by this point in history, witnessed by hundreds of people.

"Yes," an objector might say, "but witnesses lie." We have at least a couple of responses to this objection. First, we must not so quickly disregard the importance of eyewitness testimony in Jewish society. God's law required two witnesses for something as serious as the death penalty for a crime (Num. 35:30). And for good reason. This was a time before photographic evidence, so eyewitness testimony carried a greater emphasis. Witnesses were the only available means to authenticate a claim.

Even though we're far removed from this culture, we still rely on eyewitness testimony. For instance, no one reading this has ever seen Alexander the Great. We don't possess any photographs or paintings of him. But I would presume the majority of readers do not doubt his existence!

How do we know about Alexander? Only because trustworthy witnesses attested to his life. The same principle applies here. Unless we are prepared to deny the truthfulness of history before visual evidence, we must affirm the necessity of eyewitness testimony to teach us anything about the past.

Second, these witnesses had no incentive to lie about the resurrection. If they were lying, then their deception meant the loss of family, friends, job—you name it. We took note of this in chapter 2. Humanly speaking, they had every reason to say Jesus was dead and none to claim He was alive.

Therefore, we are more than justified in concluding that Paul's claims are true. Jesus was raised from the dead, and many people saw Him alive, including Paul himself. This eyewitness testimony corroborates the biblical account of the resurrection.

Resurrection and Refutation: 1 Corinthians 15:12–34

In the second major division of this chapter, Paul begins to draw out the implications of Christ's resurrection (1 Cor. 15:12–34). His argument can be summarized with relative ease. If Jesus is dead, Christianity is a hoax. But Jesus is alive. Therefore, Christianity is not a hoax. As with the first section of 1 Corinthians 15, this portion of Scripture requires careful attention to its most important details.

The elements of Paul's argument in verses 12–19 link together like a chain of inferences. The impetus for this chain was the teaching in Corinth that Jesus was not raised from the dead (v. 12). Paul reasons that if Christ was not raised, several disastrous conclusions result. First, his preaching (and, by implication, his extreme suffering for his message) is in vain (v. 14). Moreover, not only was Paul's preaching in vain, but so was the Corinthians' (and, by extension, our) faith.

Worst of all, the Apostolic message would be misrepresenting God if Christ was not raised (v. 15). Lying about God would have been an unthinkable crime for a devout (former) Jew like Paul. His reasoning here demonstrates why the resurrection is "of first importance." The very character of God hangs in the balance.

After reducing to absurdity the argument that Christ was still dead, Paul unfolds some of the implications of the resurrection. He does this in an unusual way, employing the festival calendar of ancient Israel. He signals this intention when he writes, "But in fact Christ has been raised from the dead, the firstfruits of those who have fallen asleep" (v. 20).

The term "firstfruits" is not simply an agricultural term. As we have already mentioned, it has definite religious overtones. God called ancient Israel to observe three fall festivals each year, beginning with the Feast of Trumpets, then the Day of Atonement, followed by the Feast of Booths. The three spring feasts were Passover, Firstfruits, and the Feast of Weeks, which we know in English as Pentecost (from the Greek word for "fiftieth"; see Lev. 23:1–44).

Therefore, when Paul calls Christ's resurrection the "firstfruits," he is drawing our attention to the nature of the resurrection itself. It is the beginning, just like the first gleaning of a harvest. This initial sample indicates what is to come.

As the firstfruits, Christ's resurrection indicates what kind of harvest we can expect. In this case, the yield is awe-inspiring; it is nothing less than a new creation. Paul's line of think ing here is what led the scholar we mentioned in the introduction to conclude that Christ's resurrection and our resurrection are not two separate events but two episodes of the same event. This distinction underscores the firstfruits/harvest relationship that is central to Paul's thinking in these verses.

The Mississippi Delta is a region of the state of Mississippi (roughly from the northwest corner of the state down to Vicksburg on the banks of the Mississippi River) that is home to the most fertile soil in the world. Cotton used to be the mainstay of this region, but not anymore. Still, there are a fair number of cotton growers in the delta, some of whom I have the pleasure of calling friends. I have learned a lot from them about cotton, life, and the Lord.

Among the many lessons they taught me was the importance of the firstfruits. As most of these farmers are fourth-generation, maybe fifth-generation, cotton growers, they could tell the quality of the crop by the first few bolls. Eventually, after spending a good deal of time riding around this area, while dust billowed behind the truck as we bounced along, I learned to spot good cotton.

Paul's argument is that Jesus is the firstfruits and believers are the harvest. Why would he employ this imagery? To fix our minds on the certainty of our coming resurrection in order that our faith might never be shaken. If Jesus is alive, then we will one day live again too. It is more certain than the words on this page.

Hope is where Paul takes us next. In 1 Corinthians 15:21–34, he reasons with what we might call a holy impatience. The scope of these verses is the whole of human history. Paul reminds us that resurrection has an order (v. 23), meaning that there will be a delay between the two episodes of Christ's resurrection and our resurrection.

Even with this delay, hope will not die because one day Jesus will rule the universe as King (vv. 27–29). His universal reign is part of the resurrection harvest and therefore is also as certain as the empty tomb. Before closing out this section, Paul reinforces the point he made back in verses 12–19 when he writes, "If the dead are not raised, 'Let us eat and drink, for tomorrow we die'" (v. 32).

He reiterates this truth because he doesn't want us to miss the main point. If Jesus is dead, we have no hope. We have only the here and now. And that means we're right back to the moderate nihilism we discussed in chapter 1.

We often hear variations on the idea that we ought to "eat, drink, and be merry, for tomorrow we die." This is something of a modern-day profession of faith. We are addicted to opioids and porn and drinking and food and one-night stands with strangers because we have been told that the resurrection isn't real (neither Jesus' nor our own). As a result, the beleaguered Westerner takes his seat daily in the pews of the First Church of Nothingness.

Our despairing congregant stands and recites, as it were, "There is no God; there is no resurrection; and therefore I will eat, drink, and be merry, for tomorrow I die." The First Church of Nothingness is growing at a rapid pace (witness the rise of so-called nones, those who profess no religious affiliation) and planting churches all over the place.

Paul's reasoning in this section of 1 Corinthians 15 calls us away from the endless and mindless refrain of the culture's hymns and creeds of death and despair. There are but two options for our profession of faith. We either say, "I believe in hopelessness," or we say, "I believe that Jesus is alive." This was the choice in Paul's time. It is still the choice in our time.

Resurrection and Rejuvenation: 1 Corinthians 15:35–58

The final section of 1 Corinthians 15 contains some of the most difficult teaching in the New Testament. But the main thought is easy enough to grasp. Paul teaches us, as far as has been revealed to him, the nature of the resurrection body.

He turns to the natural world to make his point. Just as animals, humans, and birds differ with respect to their flesh, so the resurrection body will be different from our current body (vv. 38–39). It will be more glorious (vv. 40–41). But, once again, resurrection has an order: "'The first man Adam became a living being'; the last Adam became a life-giving spirit. But it is not the spiritual that is first but the natural, and then the spiritual" (vv. 45–46).[3]

The biblical storyline contains an undeniable chronology. Adam lived (and died) a long time before Jesus walked the earth. Still, if we mistake Paul as simply unfolding a timeline for us in these verses, we will miss his much more significant emphasis.

Instead of merely tracing a chronology from Adam to Christ, Paul invites us to consider how history is defined by these two individuals. When he contrasts Adam and Christ, he is doing the same thing that he did in Romans 5:12–21. Both in those verses and here, Adam and Christ function as covenantal heads in Paul's theology. That means that by their actions, they represent all those who are united to them.

Consequently, Paul contrasts the body of this age (Adam's body), the body subject to death, with the body of the believer animated by the Holy Spirit. That's what he means by the spiritual body. It is the body that is indwelled by the Holy Spirit.

Generally speaking, when we see the word *spiritual* in Paul's writings, we should capitalize the *s*. That is, he does not mean *spiritual* in the modern sense of "having to do with religious ideas, convictions, practices, etc." Instead, he means *Spiritual* in the sense of "controlled by the Holy Spirit."

Therefore, in these verses, Paul caps his teaching on the nature of the resurrection body with a contrast between the body Adam (and each of us) was born with naturally and the glorified body of the coming resurrection, the body filled to the brim, as it were, with the Holy Spirit. All of this comes about at the moment we come to faith in Jesus. We cease being represented by Adam (even though we live in a physical body) and begin being represented by Christ, the "life-giving Spirit."

Why is Christ called the life-giving Spirit? Because He has been so filled with the Spirit at His resurrection (Rom. 1:4) that He is the coagent, along with the Spirit, of the prophesied new creation. That's Paul's central concern in these verses.

Let's catch our breath after that plunge into deep theological water. The basic takeaway from this discussion is that resurrection life begins now because of what Jesus has done. In other words, though resurrection of the body is future, the resurrection life of our souls starts the moment we come to Christ by faith alone. As a result, we can begin to experience heaven on earth while we wait for that reality.

This is why Paul concludes this chapter with a ringing affirmation of the certain hope we have in Christ. Death has lost its sting (1 Cor. 15:55), and Jesus has conquered both sin and death (vv. 56–57). The grand conclusion of 1 Corinthians 15 is one of my favorite Bible verses: "Therefore, my beloved brothers, be steadfast, immovable, always abounding in the work of the Lord, knowing that in the Lord your labor is not in vain" (v. 58).

Jesus' resurrection is the only thing that can make this exhortation possible. It is fundamental to everything Paul has said to this point in the chapter, and his conclusion brings this basic reality into sharp relief. Because Jesus has been raised, our faith will remain steadfast and immovable.

Not only will we press on in this life of trial and disappointment, but we will also flourish, according to the Apostle. We will be "always abounding in the work of the Lord." To borrow a cliché, we will not only survive; we will thrive.

Whenever I read this verse, one of my favorite books comes to mind. Ben Hogan, who has been described as the greatest ball-striker ever to play the game of golf, wrote a series of five articles on the golf swing for *Sports Illustrated* in the 1950s. Eventually, they were edited and released in what many consider to be the best golf instruction manual available, *Ben Hogan's Five Lessons.*

Now, my golf game has been used by the Lord to make my long-suffering golfing buddies yearn for the resurrection! Despite my (considerable) shortcomings, Hogan's book revolutionized how I play the game. He unravels the mystery of the golf swing in simple, repeatable, and accessible terms. His basic argument is that it can be mastered with practice. As a result, amateurs can play the game at a decent, enjoyable level.

Toward the end of the book, he writes about his own joy in the game. Keep in mind, he was writing at a time when the whole idea of disciplined weight lifting, coaching, and practice was just beginning to make its way into the golf world. Hogan was a pioneer in terms of his relentless practice schedule, which included hours on the course each day.

In the midst of this grueling regimen, Hogan maintained a childlike delight in the game throughout his life. In the final chapter of his book, he concludes, "I have always thought of golf as the best of all games. . . . Whether my schedule for the following day called for a tournament round or merely a trip to the practice tee, the prospect that there was going to be golf in it made me feel privileged and extremely happy and I couldn't wait for the sun to come up the next morning so that I could get out on the course again."[4]

The mentality that says "I can't wait for the sun to come up" is the mentality of resurrection. So when I think of "always abounding in the work of the Lord," I think of Hogan and the loud cracks from his persimmon woods that echoed over the hills as he practiced each day, taking delight in shot after shot.

That same kind of joy should mark our daily lives, even if we don't have the advantage of being a professional golfer. We can be "always abounding" in our workaday lives.

How is it possible to live like this? The little word *vain* tells us how. Recall Paul's reasoning from verses 12–19. If Christ is dead, our faith is "in vain." We have no hope. But because the resurrection of Christ happened, our labor in Christ is not in vain. Therefore, everything we do matters, and none of it is meaningless.

Knowing this truth and kneading it into our lives can bring such joy! The life to come colors the mundane tasks of everyday life with an eternal hue. Our work becomes a symphony of praise as we labor in our callings with the sure knowledge that God is with us and for us.

We now see clearly the main contours of Paul's thinking in this pivotal chapter. Christ's resurrection is an indicator of the coming resurrection of all believers. We do not know all the details we would like to know about our resurrection bodies, but we do know that they are united to Christ in the power of the Spirit. Tangible, lasting hope—what so many search for and so few find—follows inexorably from these truths. Those, in miniature, are Paul's central thoughts in this chapter.

THE DAY OF RESURRECTION: 1 THESSALONIANS 4:13–18

We'll look at one final resurrection text in Paul's writings to close out this chapter. In what is probably Paul's earliest letter (written around AD 50), he encourages the infant church in Thessalonica with these words:

> But we do not want you to be uninformed, brothers, about those who are asleep, that you may not grieve as others do who have no hope. For since we believe that Jesus died and rose again, even so, through Jesus, God will bring with him those who have fallen asleep. For this we declare to you by a word from the Lord, that we who are alive, who are left until the coming of the Lord, will not precede those who have fallen asleep. For the Lord himself will descend from heaven with a cry of command, with the voice of an archangel, and with the sound of the trumpet of God. And the dead in Christ will rise first. Then we who are alive, who are left, will be caught up together with them in the clouds to meet the Lord in the air, and so we will always be with the Lord. Therefore encourage one another with these words. (1 Thess. 4:13–18)

As he did in 1 Corinthians 15, Paul ministers hope in this passage. In particular, he offers spiritual relief to those struggling with the inevitable grief that death introduces into our lives. He is pastoring them by offering them true doctrine.

As an aside, the Bible never sets theological precision and pastoral comfort in contrast with one another. They are inextricably linked, and Paul demonstrates this unbreakable bond in his reasoning.

All of us can relate to the grief the Thessalonians were experiencing. When we lose a beloved friend or family member to death's icy grip, grief can paralyze us. It can consume our waking moments and steal away our sleep.

Paul understands grief's potential to ruin our lives. So, he instructs us to grieve in a certain way. We are not to grieve as those who have no hope (v. 13), as those who think that death means the end of someone forever.

Why does Paul keep bringing us back to hope? Because what we hope in reveals what we believe will save us. Our hopes tell us what we think matters most. We get through the ups and downs of life based on what we hope is coming.

Maybe it's the prospect of finally having a relationship work out. Maybe it's the hope that we will have enough money to feel secure at last. The problem with these and other hopes is that they will always let us down. That's because the moment we put our trust in them, we have exchanged the true hope of the gospel for a false hope.

Therefore, in these verses, Paul wages a worship war, with our hearts as the battlefield. When we grieve, it reveals our hope. If our grief is all-consuming and there is no turning to the Lord, then we might be hoping in the wrong things.

To help us, Paul instructs us to view our grief through the lens of Christ's resurrection (v. 14). When we do that, we begin to see, however dimly through our tears, the promise of eternal life. And as we see this promise, we can take even more comfort in the fact that Paul is giving us a "word from the Lord" (v. 15). Therefore, we know his words are true.

As Paul outlines what will happen when Christ returns at the end of all things, we learn some important details about the resurrection. First, contrary to some popular teaching in our day, Paul teaches that there is one resurrection that happens at the second coming of Jesus. The New Testament writers are unified in their declaration that the next (and final) event in redemptive history is the return of Christ. It does not occur in stages, with some resurrected and some left behind.

Second, Paul wants us to recognize the unity of God's people throughout the ages. He will transform His elect, both living and dead, by resurrection "through Christ." As one author put it, because we are "in Christ," death may interrupt our lives, but it cannot separate us eternally from God.[5]

Immediately, the connection between the passages from 1 Thessalonians and 1 Corinthians comes into focus. In both passages, death is treated as a foreign interlude to greater, ultimate life. It may be able to separate us from our bodies, but not from our God.

I don't want this to come across as morbid, but one of the greatest privileges of being a pastor is witnessing faithful Christians leave this life and enter glory. Because of passages like these, the family they leave behind expresses deep joy through the shoulder-shaking sobs. They are saddened beyond what words can express, but they know their loved one is beholding Jesus face-to-face. Nothing will ever separate the one who has died from the One who died for him.

Whether in grief or in daily life, Paul says that our joy depends on what we think about Jesus. God wants us to understand that the Savior who knows our grief so well bore our grief to the cross precisely so that grief would not have the last word. In Christ, life is eternal, but grief is not!

I once heard a pastor put it this way: when we die, we leave the land of the dying and enter the land of the living. This statement captures the essence of Paul's teaching in these verses. We can grieve well because Christ will one day make the land of the dying the land of the living—forever.

Hence, Paul closes out this passage as he did 1 Corinthians 15: with hope. He tells us to "encourage one another with these words" (1 Thess. 4:18). As we remind ourselves of these central truths, we find encouragement. Our resurrection, though still future, becomes a reality in this present life of death and heartache.

CONCLUSION

We have covered a lot of ground in this chapter. We can regain the big picture by keeping these things in mind. First, Paul reminds us that the resurrection was both predicted (by the Scriptures) and verified (by eyewitnesses). Second, Paul teaches us that there are massive, life-altering implications for denying the resurrection. Third, Paul wants us to grasp the certainty of Christ's resurrection and the glorious change our coming resurrection promises not only for us as individuals but for the entire cosmos. Believing all this helps us live productive, joy-filled lives for His glory!

Chapter Seven

FIRM HOPE

THE RESURRECTION
AND DAILY LIFE

"We're all gonna die." We've probably heard these words screamed by some hapless passenger on a hijacked vehicle in an action movie. We don't even pay attention when we hear them in that context, as we wait for the hero to show up and rescue the plane, train, or automobile. Despite this kind of familiarity, when I heard these words recently, they gave me pause.

We were sitting at the dinner table on vacation in the Lowcountry of South Carolina (which is near the coast). Though I have been going there for years, I am overcome each time by sunsets over the sparkling rivers that wend their way through endless beige marshes, tossed gently back and forth by a careless breeze, stretching ever toward the Atlantic. We were enjoying our supper looking across the May River at one of these chamber of commerce sunsets when my four-year-old blurted out, "We're all gonna die."

Of course, my wife and I were startled. We looked at each other and mouthed words, but nothing really came out. We didn't know what to say. But then our little girl took a bite of her chicken nugget. She glanced toward the ceiling, puzzling through the conundrum she had just posed, and added matter-of-factly, "But Jesus moved the stone."

As she said these words, the golden splendor of the fading sun illumined the moss hanging from the ancient oak tree outside our window. Maybe it was a child's innocent expression of both the terrifying reality of death and the soul-cheering hope of the resurrection. Maybe it was the whole scene, a moment when innocence and depth intersected as God's glory was on full display.

Whatever it was, my daughter's words made us both tear up. Her simple creed is the substance of what this book is about, the reality that death does not have the last word. The resurrection of Christ does.

Accordingly, this chapter applies what we have learned about the resurrection to our daily lives. We have explored how criticisms of the resurrection fail. We have surveyed the biblical teaching on this great subject. It remains to ask a question we ask every week in the Sunday school class I teach (stand by for another lame acronym): WDIMFM? That stands for "What does it mean for Monday?" In other words, what difference does what we have studied make for everyday living?

RESURRECTION LIFE IN THE SPIRIT
AS BELIEVERS

All Christians want to know how the past resurrection of Christ and our future resurrection in union with Him shape our everyday lives. We hinted at this in the previous chapter, but it bears repeating and expanding here. We will never see how the resurrection changes our lives until we understand that all change happens by the power of the Holy Spirit. One of our greatest privileges as Christians is being indwelled by the third person of the Trinity. Therefore, the resurrection life is the Spirit-filled life (Acts 2:4; Rom. 8:4–7; Eph. 5:18).

This Spirit-filled life cannot be considered apart from another biblical doctrine: union with Christ. A quick read of the Apostle Paul's letters reveals that his favorite expression to describe believers is not "Christians." Instead, it's a little two-word phrase: "in Christ." A follower of Jesus is someone who is "in Christ." To grasp what God is telling us, we need to take a brief detour and outline the basics of the biblical doctrine of union with Christ.

Though this doctrine had fallen on hard times in evangelicalism, theologians and authors are paying more attention to it than they have at any time in recent memory. Despite renewed interest, it is still too often misunderstood. I certainly don't promise to clear up all the confusion, but I want to sketch the doctrine's basic contours and its relationship to the resurrection.

At the most basic level, union with Christ means that by faith alone, Christ is now our representative, whereas Adam was previously our representative. As many authors have put it, union with Christ means that what is true of Jesus is now true of us (in a creaturely way, of course) by faith alone. We are born united to Adam, meaning we are born guilty and sinful (Ps. 51:5; Rom. 5:12–21). Adam's sin was imputed, or counted, to us. As a result of his first transgression, every aspect of our humanity is fallen.

Central to the good news is the reversal of this situation. As one church father put it, "Where Adam failed, Christ prevailed." Christ obeyed the law perfectly in our place (Rom. 5:12–21; 2 Cor. 5:17–21), and His obedience is imputed to us when we are united to Him by faith alone. So, the moment you put your faith in Jesus, God sees you through Christ. His account, as it were, is counted as yours.

This inseparable link between union with Christ and the resurrection is why Paul can write things like this: "For if we have been united with him in a death like his, we shall certainly be united with him in a resurrection like his" (Rom. 6:5). How could we be united to Christ's death and resurrection when we weren't alive two thousand years ago? Because faith links us to Christ's death and resurrection. Faith makes what He did true for us.

Union with Christ teaches us that, in an important sense, we are *already* resurrected with Christ. That's Paul's point in Romans 6:5. Certainly, we are not resurrected bodily yet. But we have been raised, by union with Christ, to new life in Him (John 5:24–25; Col. 3:5).

Therefore, union with Christ changes our perspective on this life entirely. As one author explains, because of this union, we live from heaven to earth, not from earth to heaven, so to speak.[1] This scholar is simply following Paul's teaching in Ephesians 2:6, where he tells us that God "raised us up with him and seated us with him in the heavenly places in Christ Jesus." Given the resurrection of Jesus, our position in the here and now is changed at the most fundamental level. This "positional reality," as we'll call it, has sweeping implications for all of life.

Not only does union with Christ help us understand the resurrection, but it explains why this life is so hard. As I was writing this chapter, I learned of the death of popular writer and blogger Rachel Held Evans. She was heralded as one of the leading voices for disillusioned evangelicals who are rethinking biblical doctrines. Although I do not share her views, her death at age thirty-seven, leaving behind a husband and two children, elicits profound sympathy.

However, I was disheartened to read the response to her illness of one of her friends and fellow "evangelical progressives," Chris Boeskool. He wrestled with the fact that so many had prayed for Evans. Struggling to come to grips with the fact that she was not coming out of her coma, he lamented:

> I guess that's my worry here: It feels to me like these prayers for healing paint a picture of a God on a throne. . . . A God who has plenty of water for a kid dying of thirst, but who is like, *"Sorry, you didn't say PLEASE."* It feels like a physician who has the cure for a deadly disease, but requires the sick person to get 10,000 signatures first. Or to get a hashtag trending. It feels like being back at that Holy Spirity, charismatic church, and having to listen to people talk about *"Storming the Gates of Heaven,"* or *"Holding God to his promises."* It feels like the bulls**t that is *"Name It & Claim It."*[2]

I sympathize with his aversion to the "prosperity gospel" (which is no gospel at all), but his comments evidence a serious misunderstanding of the character of God and the basics of prayer (not to mention unnecessary vulgarity). Union with Christ corrects this kind of confusion by showing us how suffering, glory, and resurrection are related.

Up to this point, we have only discussed how union with Christ assures us of glory and repositions us in God's sight. These are magnificent truths, and we must celebrate them. But before we witness resurrection, either for Jesus or for us, we experience suffering. If we truly want to understand union with Christ, God, prayer, and the Christian life in general, we must grasp this frightful yet necessary truth. The irreversible pattern, both for Jesus and His followers, is *suffering, then glory*.

Jesus was a "man of sorrows and acquainted with grief" (Isa. 53:3). He lived out His days on this earth misunderstood, maltreated, underhoused, unappreciated, scorned, mocked, and eventually murdered. By anyone's standard, His life was miserable.

Nonetheless, His daily sufferings had a point. They had a goal. They were for us, in two ways (Heb. 12:2). First, He lived like this as part of His work for our salvation. Second, He lived this way to show us what to expect in union with Him.

This is why one of His core teachings was cross bearing. "And he said to all, 'If anyone would come after me, let him deny himself and take up his cross daily and follow me'" (Luke 9:23). Here is Jesus' template for the Christian life. Before we are resurrected to life in glory, we suffer here below.

To get our arms around this difficult prospect, we must not read our own definition of *suffering* into the New Testament's use of the term. As one scholar explains, the word means something broader in the New Testament. He writes that suffering means not only martyrdom for one's faith but also "the mundane frustrations and unspectacular difficulties of our everyday lives when they are endured for [Jesus'] sake."[3]

I love that description because all of us can relate to it. Could we sum up our daily lives better than a series of "mundane frustrations and unspectacular difficulties"? I think these realities probably led Boeskool to voice his displeasure with God for not healing Evans.

After all, God seems absent so much of the time. Prayer seems fruitless. Loved ones die. Children go astray. Spouses lose interest in one another. Dreams fade like furniture left in the sunlight over the years. Nothing is perfect. Everything is broken.

If we do not understand that at the very center of our call to follow Christ is the call to suffer with Him, these harsh truths of everyday life will lead us to despair. At the very least, they will open the door for the kind of brash questioning that Boeskool and others throughout church history display in the face of such hardship. And though we should resonate with such disappointment, the New Testament insists we reconsider our view of the Christian life to avoid similar letdowns.

Once we come to terms with the essential role suffering plays in our union with Christ, mundane frustrations and unspectacular difficulties begin to make sense. We realize afresh the truth of Jesus' words when He said, "A disciple is not above his teacher, but everyone when he is fully trained will be like his teacher" (Luke 6:40). Suffering is a nonnegotiable aspect of our discipleship. Cross bearing is part of Christ following.

I don't intend to minimize the pain we experience at seemingly unanswered prayer. Much less do I want to downplay the agonizing grief that grips us when a friend or family member dies. But we do not honor God, and we do not help ourselves, when we shake our fist at the heavens, as though hardship and suffering are something strange. According to the Bible, they are not (1 Peter 4:12). They mean we're on the right path.

In my ministry, I have been privileged to witness Christians suffering well. Watching them endure like this has been both humbling and strengthening. They embody the truth that suffering comes before glory.

I have watched parents put the bodies of toddlers into the cold earth. I have seen faithful saints suffering horribly with diseases like pancreatic cancer. I have prayed with families struggling to come to terms with a beloved child's suicide. I leave these situations bewildered, full of questions, and with my faith stretched to the breaking point.

Through it all, I have seen firsthand families and individuals, with pain so deep that words failed them, continue to trust God. If anything, their faith has deepened in their suffering. It takes my breath away.

Their steadfast confidence in the Lord helps me fathom the unfathomable truth that, in ways none of us will understand this side of glory, suffering is God's design for our lives. The pathway to a mature, lasting faith—the type of faith that gives way to resurrection sight—is paved with the rough stones of suffering (Col. 4:12; Heb. 6:1). The only way to keep putting one foot in front of the other on this dark road is through union with Christ and with the promise of resurrection to light the way.

So, the first aspect of a Spirit-filled life is suffering unto glory in union with Christ. Here we see the Spirit manifest His power in our lives. No one but God Himself could keep us on the resurrection road when such difficulties loom in front of us. The Spirit indwells us to enable us to suffer well in union with Christ.

We Live in the Overlap of the Ages

If union with Christ explains our present experience and future hope, the next feature of a Spirit-filled life is more *structural* than *experiential*; that is, it explains the very nature of reality itself. This reality is what we discussed in the last chapter, the two-age structure of history.

We observed there that the Bible divides history into two ages: this age and the age to come. Moreover, these two ages overlap. With that in mind, we can answer this question: How do the Holy Spirit, the resurrection, and the two ages coincide?

First, this structural reality explains why evil seems to win all the time. We still live in this "present evil age" (Gal. 1:4). As a result, this world is still under the power of the devil (1 John 5:19; Rev. 20:3). He deceives the nations (Rev. 20:3, 8) and causes untold malice, cruelty, and injustice (Rev. 9:7–11). This age is the age of sin, lawlessness, and grief.

The Scriptures do not shy away from describing reality in such bleak terms. Unlike many sacred texts, the Bible takes evil seriously. It does so by pointing out, over and over again, that this world is not the way God intended it to be. Adam's sin has brought unspeakable tragedy to humanity, and we're all in on it. Therefore, until Christ returns, this present age will always be this present *evil* age.

In the second place, the two-age structure of reality tells us how we can still know true joy despite the fallen world in which we live. Paul tell us why. "So we do not lose heart. Though our outer man is wasting away, our inner man is being renewed day by day" (2 Cor. 4:16, author's translation). This verse links the resurrection, the work of the Spirit, and the two ages to daily Christian experience. It is one of the most significant verses in the Bible.

According to God's Word here, the resurrection of Christ inaugurated the age to come in this present evil age. Our resurrection in union with Christ will mark the end of this age and the beginning of the age to come. The coming resurrection of the dead is what separates the two ages. In between, our outer man is subject to death and sin, but the resurrection of the inner man exemplifies the overlap of the two ages.

We need to be clear that when Paul distinguishes between the outer man and the inner man, he does not mean that our outer man is our bodies and our inner man is our souls. Instead, the outer man refers to life in this age, while the inner man refers to the resurrected person, "the real us," which only comes to completion at the last day. Hence, though we have been resurrected in Christ in the inner man, we still live in this life in the outer-man reality of death and decay.

The tension between the inner/outer-man dynamic marks out every step of our earthly journey. If we do not experience the renewal of the inner man by the power of the Spirit, our circumstances will grind us into powder. The outer-man reality will destroy us, as it were.

Moreover, this distinction highlights what theologians call the "already/not yet" tension that characterizes the overlap of the two ages. Put concretely, we are already resurrected but not yet bodily. Or, to use another example, Jesus has already triumphed over death, but we do not yet see that triumph in its fullness.

Now, all of this talk about inner/outer-man dynamics may strike many readers as unnecessarily heady. But a right understanding of Paul's meaning here makes all the difference in the world, as a friend of mine illustrates.

For most of his ministry, he was imprisoned in a country that was hostile to the gospel. Separated from his family and tortured for believing in Jesus, he passed his days in a prison cell with no light, no communication, and, if viewed purely from an "outer man" perspective, no hope.

In the face of these difficulties, he continued to trust God. As I sat with him over a meal one evening as he described his time in jail, his eyes burned with characteristic intensity when he grabbed my arm and said: "It was in that prison cell that the Lord drew near to me. I had joy." This kind of faith seems impossible to many of us. Yet here was a man who understood this tension and was being renewed in the inner man.

What is the Spirit's role in this inner-man/outer-man dynamic? The short answer is that He is the effective agent of this renewal-resurrection (1 Cor. 15:45). Jesus, by the Spirit, is "making all things new" in us and, ultimately, in the world He created (Rev. 21:5).

With this in mind, we can begin to see how the Holy Spirit changes our lives between the two ages. He is resurrecting us as we more and more come to enjoy and live out our union with Christ. He is the Spirit of the age to come (Rev. 22:17) bringing that future glory into the midst of this present evil age, in our daily lives.

All of this happens by faith and by faith alone. We do not yet see these glories fully realized. Hence, "we walk by faith, not by sight" (2 Cor. 5:7). Appearances to the contrary, the Spirit's activity of resurrection in this life will one day give way to a resurrected cosmos. As a result of the Spirit's work, we can have deep, lasting joy, even if our circumstances are anything but joyful, as my friend's testimony makes plain.

The scope of Paul's thought here is stunning. He has brought union with Christ, resurrection, and world history together in this one verse. History is headed toward resurrection. Until that day, believers have the privilege of being Spirit-filled, daily resurrected witnesses to the power of Christ as they suffer in union with Him.

This is why our daily lives matter more than we can possibly imagine. As we walk in union with Christ, we are microcosms, as it were, of history. Our daily resurrection in Christ by the Spirit points forward to the time when the inner-man reality of resurrection will swallow up the outer-man bondage to decay and death. Daily disappointment is thus transformed into a beacon of ceaseless hope!

The main point of all that we have said so far is that life in the Spirit is life between the ages, in union with Christ. For us as individual believers, nothing could be more glorious or more satisfying. Next, we will explore some implications of Christ's resurrection for the life of the church.

RESURRECTION LIFE IN THE SPIRIT AS THE CHURCH

As necessary and indispensable as individual transformation is, the Bible teaches that life in the Spirit is not limited to our own private experience. It is a communal reality.

The local church has fallen on hard times. Radicals deny her necessity; everyone sees her inconsistencies. Despite her tattered appearance in the eyes of a watching world, the church, in its local and global expressions, is still the bride of Christ. He loves her more than we will ever fathom. In her rags of disobedience, failure, and shame, she is still incomparably beautiful to Him (Eph. 5:25).

Therefore, at the center of history is not just individual resurrection but the coming resurrection of God's people, the church. The church is at the center of God's plan for the universe (Acts 20:28; Eph. 1:22–23).

Maybe you have been wounded horribly by the church. Maybe you've given up on her. I understand. The church can devour her own—and those outside—like few other institutions. Despite this hard fact, please keep reading. Because so many people have been hurt in and by the church and her leadership, we need to draw a vital biblical distinction before we go any further.

The distinction I have in mind is between the visible and invisible church (Matt. 7:21–23; 13:24–30; 1 John 2:19–20). The visible church is all those who profess the faith of Jesus and their children (my Presbyterianism is showing!). The invisible church is made up of the elect around the world through the ages. So, someone can be a member of the visible church without being a member of the invisible church. As the old hymn put it, sadly the church has "false sons in her pale."[4] In different terms, just because someone goes to church is no guarantee that he is a Christian.

Therefore, when I use the word *church*, I am referring to the elect of God, those who are truly His. The resurrection of Christ was for His people, the church. Therefore, we cannot think about the resurrection without discussing its ramifications for the Spirit-indwelled community.

Resurrection Power Equips the Church for Her Mission

When we were first married, I wanted to impress my wife by installing a new tile floor in our kitchen. Mind you, I had never done any tile work in my life. So, like any good DIY-er, I logged on to YouTube. "Nothing to it," I thought to myself, after watching some videos.

I proceeded to tear up the old floor. So far, so good. I purchased the amount of tile I needed, along with backer board and bags of grout, and embarked on my floor upgrade. "Chip Gaines. Whatever," I muttered, smiling.

About fifteen minutes into attempting to measure, cut, and place the tile, I realized I was in over my head. With admirable restraint, my dear wife suggested I might get some help for my floor makeover. With a delicious slice of humble pie spilling over my plate, I phoned one of the deacons from our church, the kind of guy who can fix or build anything.

He came over the next day and backed his truck carefully down our steep driveway. He swung down the tailgate and selected the necessary tools to tile the floor correctly. We set up shop and got to work and within a day, the extensive mess I had made of our kitchen actually looked decent.

Here's the point. We need to be equipped properly to complete our mission. The resurrection of Jesus gives us all that we'll ever need to live for Him faithfully in this life. It equips and empowers us to do what the Lord has called us to do.

How does the resurrection of Jesus equip the church for her

mission? Primarily, through *the outpouring of the Holy Spirit.* Once again, redemption has a logical order to it. The Father raises Jesus from the dead, He ascends to heaven, and the Spirit descends upon His people—all as the Old Testament prophesies (Isa. 61:1–4; Eze. 36:26; Joel 2:28–32).

Since the moment the Spirit descended upon the church at Pentecost (Acts 2:1–4), He has remained with her for all time. As an aside, the interworking of the Father, Son, and Spirit in the mission of the church displays the unity of purpose and mission among the persons of the Trinity for all the world to see. Salvation is Trinitarian from start to finish!

Modern evangelicals tend to err in one of two directions regarding the work of the Spirit in the life of the church. On the one hand, *He is put at the center when He Himself would recede into the background.* In this approach, what matters more than anything for the church is that she manifests the supernatural gifts of the Spirit. If the church isn't doing this, she's not being faithful, according to proponents of this approach.

Without entering the thorny debate concerning the nature and extent of the gifts of the Spirit (1 Cor. 12:1–31) in our day and age, we can say at least this much. As one author put it so memorably, the Spirit's primary task in the church is to act as a spotlight. He points away from Himself to Christ. As a result, for the Spirit to exalt Himself to the detriment of the Father and the Son would be contrary to His stated mission (John 16:13–15).

On the other hand is something equally dangerous: an *underappreciation* of the Spirit's ministry to God's people. Generally speaking, this approach is a reaction to the previous misstep. It attempts to correct those who would overexalt the Spirit's presence by (no doubt, unintentionally) limiting His role in the life of the church.

The scriptural balance between these two extremes can be hard to discern. What is clear, however, is that the outpouring of the Spirit on the church equips God's people for effective witness (Acts 1:8); fervent, Spirit-dominated prayer (Rom. 8:26–27); and warfare against our three main enemies: the world, the flesh, and the devil (Eph. 6:18).

Therefore, the church's empowerment by the ascension of Jesus and the outpouring of the Spirit is for all believers. It is not limited only to those who have experienced a special "baptism of the Holy Spirit." The biblical data specifies that God's design is for all who are united to Christ to be filled with the Spirit. The two are inseparable; if we are Christ's, we are the Spirit's, and He is in us.

Having been resurrected in the inner man and being indwelled by the Spirit, we are sent by God to fulfill His mission for the church. He will never leave us nor forsake us (Matt. 28:20; Heb. 13:5). In the resurrection of Christ and the outpouring of the Holy Spirit, the church has all she needs to accomplish the purpose God has for her.

The Church's Primary Calling Is Evangelism and Discipleship

Our discussion to this point raises a fundamental question: What is the mission of the church? A full answer would require a book in itself.[5] Nonetheless, we will need to consider a basic response to this question.

We must first realize what the church's primary calling is *not*. Her highest calling is not social transformation (more on this below). Her primary mission is not to overthrow worldly institutions. In a word, the church's mission is not focused on this age. Instead, the church's task is, above all, evangelism and discipleship (Matt. 28:18–20). Jesus made this clear at the outset of His ministry when He said, "Let us go onto the next towns, that I may preach there also, for that is why I came out" (Mark 1:38).

This focus on the church's mission may come as a surprise to some readers, so let me try to clarify what I'm saying. Should Christians love the poor and seek to serve them in any way they can? Absolutely. Should Christians seek the welfare of the cities in which they find themselves (Jer. 29:7), working to better the schools, government, and overall quality of life in that area? Yes.

But these kinds of activities, which are simply aspects of discipleship to the Lord, are subservient to the overall mission of the church. When we serve at a soup kitchen or bring lifesaving water to the developing world, if we are being faithful to Jesus' mission, we do so in the hopes of seeing people become disciples of Jesus. From the biblical standpoint, we must be just as concerned about someone's eternal destiny as we are that they enjoy temporal necessities (Matt. 16:26; John 6:27). Focusing on one at the expense of the other leads us away from the gospel balance.

Again, just to be clear, Christians must and should abound in concern for the poor, the forgotten, and the marginalized. Faith devoid of good works is worthless (James 2:17). Yet, we must remember that these good works serve the greater purpose of Christ's church, which is evangelism and discipleship.

Therefore, the church's primary task is not cultural transformation, as so many have argued throughout church history, but faithfulness to Christ's mission. Since His resurrection, the Lord has used such faithfulness to transform the world around His people. Still, this kind of change ebbs and flows. The only kind of change that lasts is the renewal of the inner man, which will one day culminate in the renewal of the cosmos. Until then, we keep our focus on the church's central mission.

At the core of this dual emphasis in her mission is the fact of the resurrection of Christ. In evangelism, we call people to believe in the resurrected Messiah. In discipleship, we call believers to live out their resurrection lives in union with the resurrected Christ. To that end, we need to say a few more words about the nature of this life.

RESURRECTION LIFE IN THE SPIRIT IN THIS PRESENT EVIL AGE

One of Jesus' greatest promises is that He came to give us abundant life (John 10:10). When we consider His teachings as a whole, we learn that abundant life is Spirit-filled, resurrection life. Sadly, I think many believers would describe their lives as anything but abundant. More often than not, we wander through life, wondering what it all means.

When we feel this way, the resurrection of Christ speaks to our deepest longings. We can begin where we are, right now, and experience abundant life. As we saw earlier, Jesus has given us everything we need to live for Him today. What does that look like?

We Read Prayerfully and Meditate Carefully on Scripture

We will never enjoy our union with Christ or experience the abundant life He promised if we do not become students of His

Word. The Word of God is a priceless treasure (Ps. 119:162) that a lot of us leave safely neglected on a shelf! However, when we take it down, open it up, and begin to read it in a posture of humility and prayer, resurrection life begins to pour forth from its pages (John 5:24).

Consequently, overstating the importance of regular Bible study is probably impossible. To be sure, we won't get a spiritual high every time we read it. We will have seasons when we don't feel a thing. Still, the resurrection life is inevitably connected with faithful Bible reading. That is to say, even when we don't perceive it to be "working," God's Word is always changing us, every time we read it, just as He promised us (Isa. 55:10–11).

It's similar to what we hear every time we fly. The video or the flight attendant explains that in case of emergency, oxygen masks will deploy. Then we're told not to worry if we don't see the yellow bag inflating, for oxygen is still flowing, even if it doesn't look like it. I've always thought that if I were ever on a flight where oxygen masks deployed, I'm pretty sure that whether the little yellow bag was inflating would be the least of my concerns.

In this admittedly imperfect analogy, Scripture is like those oxygen masks. Life is flowing even if we don't see it while we read. Our part is to keep reading, keep praying, and keep thinking about the Word of God.

That brings me to the whole idea of meditating carefully on Scripture. Once a staple of biblical discipleship to Jesus, meditating on Scripture is a lost art today. Mostly that's because we live such frantic, breakneck lifestyles. A friend of mine likes to say, when someone asks how he's doing, "Mach 3 with my hair on fire."

When we talk about meditating on Scripture, don't picture someone seated in the lotus position, eyes closed, chanting "om." That kind of meditation, which is meant to empty our minds in order to achieve oneness with the universe, is the very opposite of what Scripture means when it calls us to meditate on God's Word day and night (Ps. 1:2).

Instead, meditating on the Bible is more like sanctified worry, as one author put it. When we worry about something, we think it through from a variety of angles, consider possible outcomes, and contemplate our responses. The problem is, worry does nothing for us except increase our chances of an early grave.

By contrast, biblical meditation means doing what we do when we worry, only with Scripture. We take a verse or passage and think it through. We ask what it teaches us about Jesus, God, creation, and so on. We consider what it is calling us to do. We step back and look at it from a different standpoint. Put simply, biblical meditation just means thinking hard and often about the Bible.

Anyone reading this can meditate on Scripture. It is not only for the privileged elite but for every Christian. As we engage in this time-honored practice, we will begin to experience abundant life. Our hearts will overflow with God's Word, and our lives will overflow with resurrection life!

We Worship Jesus with His People

Crucial to experiencing resurrection life is regular, corporate worship with God's people. Space forbids a defense of the biblical distinction between corporate worship and all of life as worship, but it's there (see Rom. 12:1; 1 Cor. 10:31). For the moment, we will outline how corporate worship helps us experience resurrection life.

Scripture prioritizes public worship for at least two reasons. The first is the example of Jesus. Luke tells us that it was our Lord's custom to gather with God's people in the synagogue (Luke 4:16). We can easily forget that Jesus ministered publicly for only about three years. Before that, He worked and worshiped in what was considered an obscure, backwoods village in the vast Roman Empire.

So, for about thirty years, Jesus went to the synagogue at least every week. Day in, day out, week in, week out. When I consider Jesus getting up, going to work, sweating, going about His life, and then taking a day off to worship God, I am floored. The Son of God, God in the flesh, went to a dusty first-century synagogue, prayed, sang, and listened to sermons from the Old Testament.

For certain, Jesus communed with His Father privately (Matt. 14:23; Mark 1:35). But He never set His private worship of His Father at odds with His weekly gathering to worship with fellow believers. Both marked His life. Both should mark ours.

Second, in heaven, corporate worship has priority. Although we will all be worshiping as individuals in glory, this will take place in the context of the whole host of the redeemed (Rev. 5:8–14). Jesus teaches us that one of our consistent prayers should be for God's will to be done on earth as it is in heaven (Matt. 6:10). One of the ways that prayer is answered is in corporate worship.

Therefore, if we want to experience the resurrection life promised in God's Word, we must make gathering with His people for worship one of our main priorities. When we do, we are encouraged, strengthened, edified, and prepared for life in this age. It is practicing for heaven, as it were. Above all, God is glorified when we worship Him!

We Serve in the Power Jesus Supplies

Finally, we live out our resurrection life in union with Christ as we serve in the power that Jesus supplies through His Spirit (John 15:5; Eph. 3:20). With so many activities and good things calling for our attention, we always face the constant threat of burnout in our lives. We will only avoid this if we serve in the power Jesus supplies.

So how do we serve in the power Jesus supplies to us by His Spirit? First, *we face the idol of pleasing people.* Most of us who struggle with this particular idol don't even know it. Here are some symptoms: you are terrified of failure, you feel like you can never say no, you are overcommitted, and you wonder constantly what people think of you. Sound familiar? I know it does for me.

The way forward is turning from this idol and finding our security in Christ. Instead of serving people because we need them to like us and approve of us, we begin serving them because we love Jesus. He becomes our focus, not them.

Second, *we regain control of our schedules.* We are all "crazy busy." But did God intend for us to live a life of constant errands, appointments, practices, and overwork? I don't think so. Circumstances may dictate that some days we may have to do more, and some people have to work longer hours than others. And I sympathize with the desire to make sure our children are involved in activities that will help build them up in Christ. But all of us are in control of our schedules.

How do we determine what should take priority in our

commitments? We ask a simple question: "How does this help me serve Jesus?" And then we get brutally honest with ourselves. If it doesn't help us do that, we get rid of it.

That may sound hopelessly naive, but as we practice this habit, I think we'll find that we're doing less yet achieving more. Above all, by clearing away the brush from our schedules, we can see Jesus more clearly. And the more we see Him, enjoy Him, and commune with Him, the more we serve in the power of His Spirit.

Third, *we stop multitasking*. Research indicates that multitasking actually makes us less, not more, productive.[6] Moreover, as Christians, we cannot multitask prayer and Bible study, for example. Both require our undivided attention.

If our most important relationship, the one we enjoy with our heavenly Father, requires our total focus, then so also do our human relationships. Multitasking inhibits our ability to listen well and to devote ourselves to becoming students of other people. As a result, we find ourselves never getting beyond the surface in our relationships, whether with God or with others. Because we can't concentrate, we can't go deep.

But God wants us to go deep with Him and with others. The only way this happens is when we learn that doing a bunch of things runs the risk of having important things not receive our full attention. To be clear, I realize there are times when multitasking is unavoidable. What I am advocating is that a life of distracted multitasking should not be the norm for Christians. As with many parts of the Christian life, this is not easy (I know that all too well), but we still should strive to focus on Bible study, prayer, relationships, and the other things that mark the life of a Christian.

Resurrection life is a life of focused communion with God and service to others. There are no hacks. We can't take a shortcut to a profound relationship with God and deep, lasting relationships with others. They both take time and concentration. When we devote ourselves to these high callings, we will experience resurrection life. We will live in the power Christ supplies.

A common theme weaves its way through all these suggestions: the call to dependence. Here's how Jesus expressed this theme: "Truly, I say to you, unless you turn and become like children, you will never enter the kingdom of heaven" (Matt. 18:3). In other words, we may look like individuals who have it all together and crush it every day. But God wants something different for us than just being high achievers.

His goal and design for our lives is that we learn—through painful experiences, failed dreams, relational disappointments, suffering, and a host of other means—that a life of Spirit-filled power only comes as we find ourselves in a position of utter dependence on Him.

This is the lesson Paul learned in his extensive sufferings (2 Cor. 11:23–29). This toil and hardship never obscured his joy in Christ, which is why he could write: "For the sake of Christ, then, I am content with weaknesses, insults, hardships, persecutions, and calamities. For when I am weak, then I am strong" (12:10).

Complete dependence is what Jesus has in mind when He calls us to become like little children. He wants us to be humble, dependent, and singular in our devotion to our Father, through Him, in the power of the Spirit. He will do whatever it takes to bring us to this position because He loves us.

Therefore, resurrection life for the believer is hard but not joyless. It is full of disappointments and victories. Through it all, Jesus remains with us, the Spirit resurrecting us daily, all to the glory of God!

CONCLUSION

No matter what else has happened or will happen in this world, the best news ever is that the resurrection of Jesus is true. For believers, the reality of Jesus' resurrection means that everything has changed. It is an explosion of symphonic beauty that interrupts the otherwise monotonous drone of death. It is the reason the Christian keeps going. It is the fuel of hope, the fire of missions, the promise of eternity, the glorious beginning of the end we always hoped for, and the only way to make sense of the world.

ACKNOWLEDGMENTS

I owe so much to so many for making this book possible. First, to the session and members of First Presbyterian Church in Columbia, S.C., thank you for your patience with me and for being one of the finest places in the world to minister God's Word. Also, thank you to the session, staff, and membership of First Presbyterian Church in Jackson, Miss., for your continued love and encouragement.

To my pastor, Dr. Derek W.H. Thomas, thank you and your dear wife for modeling what leadership and ministry look like, day in and day out.

To the Sunday school class I have the joy of teaching each week, the Gateway class, thank you for letting me beta test some of this material on you!

Special thanks goes to the father-son duo of Lanny and Grayson Lambert for their editorial work on this volume, which was nothing short of Herculean. The remaining errors are all mine, but, to the extent this book is at all enjoyable, the credit goes to them.

To dear friends and mentors including Bill and Leigh Anne Moore, George and Cathy May, Lee and Lisa Paris, Bill and Lou Ann Harper, Jimmy and Betsy Easterby, J.R. and Aimee Murphy,

Joe and Tracie Walker, Brian Habig, Rick Phillips, Carlton Wynne, Ligon Duncan, Melton Duncan, Chris Hill, and too many others to name, thank you for teaching me more about the resurrection life than I could ever put on paper.

To Bruce and Jane Keller, thank you for loving our family well and for the many memories we share at your home!

To my brothers, parents, and extended family, thank you for everything. I love y'all more than I can ever say.

To Thomas Brewer, Kevin D. Gardner, Chris Larson, Burk Parsons, and the team at Ligonier Ministries and Reformation Trust, I am deeply grateful for this opportunity. From start to finish, this has been one of the most enjoyable projects I've been a part of. That's due to your professionalism, encouragement, and, above all, Christian love.

Finally, thanks be to the Father, Son, and Holy Spirit for my wife and children. Apart from Jesus' gift of salvation, they are the greatest gifts I have ever received in this life, a daily reminder of the goodness of the Lord. *Soli Deo gloria!*

NOTES

Introduction

1   See, for example, the seminal work of Peter Jones, *The Other Worldview: Exposing Christianity's Greatest Threat* (Bellingham, Wash.: Kirkdale, 2015).

2   Richard B. Gaffin Jr., *Resurrection and Redemption: A Study in Soteriology* (Phillipsburg, N.J.: P&R, 1987), 40.

3   I am indebted to a number of different scholars for the language of "distinct and inseparable" used here.

Chapter One

1   Richard Lewontin, "Billions and Billions of Demons," *The New York Review of Books*, January 9, 1997 (emphasis original).

2   Alex Rosenberg, *The Atheist's Guide to Reality: Enjoying Life without Illusions* (New York: W.W. Norton, 2011), 3. I first heard about this book shortly after its release in a lecture by Dr. James Anderson, and I am indebted to him for drawing my attention to it.

3   Gary R. Habermas, "Explaining Away Jesus' Resurrection: The Recent Revival of Hallucination Theories," *Christian Research Journal* 23 no. 4 (2001).

4   Martin Hengel, *Crucifixion* (Philadelphia: Fortress, 1977), 30–31.

5   Habermas, "Explaining Away Jesus' Resurrection."

6   See Michael Licona, *The Resurrection of Jesus: A New Historiographical Approach* (Downers Grove, Ill.: IVP Academic, 2010), 464–559.

7   Licona, *The Resurrection of Jesus*, for these three answers to objections.

8   John Shelby Spong, *Resurrection: Myth or Reality? A Bishop's Search for the Origin of Christianity* (San Francisco: HarperSanFrancisco, 1994), 233.

9   Spong, *Resurrection*, 254.

10   Spong, *Resurrection*, 255.

11   Spong presents his argument in *Resurrection*, 33–46.

12 Sir Frederic Kenyon, cited in Paul D. Wegner, *The Journey from Texts to Translations: The Origin and Development of the Bible* (Grand Rapids, Mich.: Baker Academic, 1999), 234.

13 Spong, *Resurrection*, 238.

14 William Lane Craig and Bart Ehrman, "Is There Historical Evidence for the Resurrection of Jesus? The Craig-Ehrman Debate," Reasonable Faith with William Lane Craig, March 2006, accessed January 2, 2019, https://www.reasonablefaith.org/media/debates/is-there-historical-evidence-for-the-resurrection-of-jesus-the-craig-ehrman.

15 Peter J. Williams, *Can We Trust the Gospels?* (Wheaton, Ill.: Crossway, 2018), 111. See pp. 53–86 for his argument regarding the accurate local knowledge evidenced in the Gospels.

16 Ehrman, in "Is There Historical Evidence?"

17 Ehrman, in "Is There Historical Evidence?"

18 R.C. Sproul, John Gerstner, and Arthur Lindsley, *Classical Apologetics: A Rational Defense of the Christian Faith and a Critique of Presuppositional Apologetics* (Grand Rapids, Mich.: Academie, 1984), 152.

Chapter Two

1 Licona, *The Resurrection of Jesus*, 371.

2 C.S. Lewis, *The Chronicles of Narnia* (New York: HarperCollins, 2001), 131.

3 "The Autobiography of Charles Darwin," March 13, 2004, accessed March 12, 2019, http://www.darwin-literature.com/The_Autobiography_of_Charles_Darwin/8.html.

4 Licona, *The Resurrection of Jesus*, 242.

5 Cited in Licona, *The Resurrection of Jesus*, 243.

6 Cited in N.T. Wright, *The Resurrection of the Son of God: Christian Origins and the Question of God* (Minneapolis, Minn.: Fortress, 2003), 3:485.

7 Wright, *The Resurrection of the Son of God*, 3:484.

Chapter Three

1 Cornelis P. Venema, *The Promise of the Future* (Carlisle, Pa.: Banner of Truth Trust, 2000), 54–55.

2 I am indebted to Dr. James Anderson for his suggestions and refinement of my original argument. All remaining mistakes in the statement of the argument are, of course, my own.

Chapter Four

1 Craig S. Keener, *The Gospel of Matthew: A Socio-Rhetorical Commentary* (Grand Rapids, Mich.: Eerdmans, 2009), 699.

2 Keener, *The Gospel of Matthew*, 698.

3 Geerhardus Vos, *Grace and Glory: Sermons Preached in the Chapel of Princeton Seminary* (Vestavia Hills, Ala.: Solid Ground, 2007), 102.

Chapter Five

1 John Lynch, "45 of the Worst Movie Sequels of All Time, Ranked by How Awful They Were," *Business Insider*, April 12, 2018, accessed April 12, 2019, https://www.businessinsider.com/worst-movie-sequels-all-time-critics-2018-4.

2 I am indebted to Dr. J. Ligon Duncan III for drawing my attention to this line of reasoning.

Chapter Six

1 Anthony C. Thiselton, *The First Epistle to the Corinthians*, New International Greek Testament Commentary (Grand Rapids, Mich.: Eerdmans, 2000), 1186.

2 See John M. Frame, *The Doctrine of the Knowledge of God* (Phillipsburg, N.J.: P&R, 1987), 130.

3 In my exegesis of these verses, readers familiar with his work will detect the controlling influence of Richard B. Gaffin Jr.'s theology on my thinking, specifically his article "'Life-Giving Spirit': Probing the Center of Paul's Pneumatology," *JETS* 41 no. 4 (December 1998): 573–89.

4 Ben Hogan with Herbert Warren Wind and drawings by Anthony Ravielli, *Ben Hogan's Five Lessons: The Modern Fundamentals of Golf* (New York: Simon & Schuster, 2006), 108–9.

5 Michael W. Holmes, *1 & 2 Thessalonians* (Grand Rapids, Mich.: Zondervan Academic, 1998), 149.

Chapter Seven

1 William D. Dennison, *In Defense of the Eschaton: Essays in Reformed Apologetics,* ed. James Douglas Baird (Eugene, Ore.: Wipf & Stock, 2015), 107.

2 Chris Boeskool, "Thoughts on Praying for Miracles," *The Boeskool*, May 1, 2019, accessed May 7, 2019, https://theboeskool.com/2019/05/01/thoughts-on-praying-for-miracles (emphasis original).

3 Gaffin, "Life-Giving Spirit," 588.

4 Samuel J. Stone, "The Church's One Foundation," 1866.

5   For one of the best popular treatments available, see Kevin DeYoung and
    Greg Gilbert, *What Is the Mission of the Church? Making Sense of Social
    Justice, Shalom, and the Great Commission* (Wheaton, Ill.: Crossway, 2011).
6   Adam Gorlick, "Media Multitaskers Pay Mental Price, Stanford Study
    Shows," *Stanford News*, August 24, 2009, accessed May 16, 2019, https://
    news.stanford.edu/news/2009/august24/multitask-research-study-082409
    .html.

SCRIPTURE INDEX

ABOUT THE AUTHOR

Dr. Gabriel N.E. Fluhrer is associate minister of discipleship at the First Presbyterian Church in Columbia, S.C., and visiting lecturer in systematic theology at Reformed Theological Seminary in Atlanta. Dr. Fluhrer previously served as church planter and founding pastor of Shiloh Presbyterian Church in Raleigh, N.C., and as minister of discipleship at First Presbyterian Church in Jackson, Miss. He has earned degrees from the University of South Carolina (B.A.), Greenville Presbyterian Theological Seminary (M.Div.), and Westminster Theological Seminary (Ph.D.) and is editor of several books, including *Atonement* and *Solid Ground*.

TRUTHFORLIFE®

THE BIBLE-TEACHING MINISTRY OF **ALISTAIR BEGG**

The mission of Truth For Life is to teach the Bible with clarity and relevance so that unbelievers will be converted, believers will be established, and local churches will be strengthened.

Daily Program

Each day, Truth For Life distributes the Bible teaching of Alistair Begg across the U.S. and in several locations outside of the U.S. through 1,800 radio outlets. To find a radio station near you, visit **truthforlife.org/stationfinder**.

Free Teaching

The daily program, and Truth For Life's entire teaching archive of over 2,000 Bible-teaching messages, can be accessed for free online and through Truth For Life's full-feature mobile app. Download the free mobile app at **truthforlife.org/app** and listen free online at **truthforlife.org**.

At-Cost Resources

Books and full-length teaching from Alistair Begg on CD, DVD, and USB are available for purchase at cost, with no markup. Visit **truthforlife.org/store**.

Where to Begin?

If you're new to Truth For Life and would like to know where to begin listening and learning, find starting point suggestions at **truthforlife.org/firststep**. For a full list of ways to connect with Truth For Life, visit **truthforlife.org/subscribe**.

Contact Truth For Life

P.O. Box 398000 Cleveland, Ohio 44139
phone 1 (888) 588-7884   **email** letters@truthforlife.org
 /truthforlife   @truthforlife   truthforlife.org